Running with Mercy

By
Robert T. Gamba

Order this book online at www.trafford.com
or email orders@trafford.com

Most Trafford titles are also available at major online book retailers.

Printed in the United States of America.

ISBN: 978-1-4120-0243-1 (sc)

Trafford rev. 02/03/2011

 www.trafford.com

North America & International
toll-free: 1 888 232 4444 (USA & Canada)
phone: 250 383 6864 ♦ fax: 812 355 4082

*The name of the Lord is a
Strong tower; the righteous
run into it and are safe.
Proverbs 18:10*

Mercy

Being justified freely by His grace through the redemption that is in Christ Jesus. Romans 3:24

Paul's letter to the Roman believers is a good place to start in understanding the mercy of God. This epistle explains the law of sin and death and eternal life with Christ.

Moses was given the letter of the law so we could understand that since Adam had failed, we have all been infected by a spiritual virus called sin that resulted in spiritual and natural death. So does that mean we are doomed and cursed for eternity, forever in a fallen state? No! God, in His loving mercy has provided a way, not twenty ways, not ten ways and not two ways, but one way to redemption from the curse of the law of sin and death. Given freely by His mercy, compassion, and His love for His creation, God shows us the depths of His grace in His forgiving power of redeeming love. The Word of God, His very nature became a Man, and in this Man was and is the Creator reconciling His creation unto Himself. One Man has recovered the fallen state of humanity just as it had fallen by the offense of one man. God's desire is for all to be saved, and His arms are out-stretched to even those that drift further away from His love. God gives and forgives because His very nature is love. However, there are conditions to His forgiveness, a channel in which His mercy flows, which is by faith in His Son, Jesus Christ, who alone paid the price for our sin with His own blood on the altar of a cross.

"So I say to you, ask and it will be given to you; seek and you will find; knock and it will be opened to you." Luke 11:9

Jesus teaches us to ask in faith and it will be given. We do have a responsibility to ask, and ask with the correct motives. So if we do not ask, if we do not seek and if we do not knock, how then can we expect to be given, expect to find, or expect the door to be opened? What will we find after we seek and knock? We will find that God's *mercy endures forever* through Jesus Christ. We can know and live in the most powerful force ever known to any being, which is the Spirit of God. We can quickly discover that even when we ran from Him, His hand of mercy was still out to us. Even when we had decided to go our own way, ignore the love of our Creator and make ourselves our own god in our own kingdom of selfishness, His mercy still endured.

For His mercy endures forever. Psalm 118: Throughout the Scriptures, God's mercy by the power of His love shines through the clouds of our fallen nature. His mercy was manifested through the lives of the people we read about in the Bible. We also have a testimony of the mercy that God has shown us, which leads through the doors of forgiveness, faith and peace. This understanding can bring us to a place of submission to His love, by the transforming power of His Spirit. However, without the acceptance of His sacrifice for our sin, we can never know the depths of His love because we are blinded by the darkness of sin, unable to perceive the light of His grace. Without God's merciful salvation we are chained in a cell of judgment lacking the power to reach God's redemption for our lives and surrounded by the walls of shame that hold us captive to the outcome of sin. This hopeless state breeds negativity, resentment and bitterness because without God, sin reigns in our weakened souls. However, *God's mercy endures forever.* God loves us too much to leave us in a fallen state of error!

When reading the following pages, remember that God's mercy, which is empowered by His love, is everlasting, without end. His love for us was revealed to all creation by the birth, life, death and resurrection of a Man who submitted His all to reunite the creation back to the Creator. This is the greatest evidence of God's mercy. The prophets were foretold of this display of love long before it took place. In the subjects touched on in this book, we will realize that without the mercy of God there would be no redemption, and no eternal life. It is only by God's extended hand of grace that we can receive all the eternal riches that are in Christ Jesus. Jesus, being the Corner Stone of His love; the path in which the mercy of God has been manifested toward us. A true encounter with His love will transform any life from the fallen state of sin and death, to the overcoming victory of eternal life. For God's mercy toward us is so strong, it even overcame sin and death!

Running

...All the runners run...

...Let us lay aside every weight, and the sin which so easily entangles us, and let us run with endurance the race that is before us.

1ˢᵗ Corinthians 9:24, Hebrews 12:1

In a world that chases after the cheap thrills of sin, the Christian life is considered old fashioned and out of touch with the newest move of the imagination of man. Many call the Christian life, the Christian walk, but I really like what God revealed to the Apostle Paul, it is a race! It is a race against every opposition that is contrary to God, a race against our short stay here called time, which ticks away second by second, and a race through the enemy's roadblocks that attempt to derail our faith in the Creator. Moreover, as in any race, all that participate must run. This is not a race of simple competition, but a run of faith, a race of a new life in Christ.

Like the marathon runner, to run in this race there will be some sacrifices, some work and some growing pains that comes with any development, which is a transformation from a death to life, even life eternal. There are no spectators in the Christian life; we all have a part to play, a job to perform, and a task of faith. This is by no means saying that one must work for his or her salvation of eternal life with Jesus Christ. What a silly thought, to think that we could add anything to the cross and the finished work of God through Jesus Christ. We can only begin to enter this race once we have eternal salvation, once we have been redeemed by the sacrifice of Christ.

The race of faith is not dependent on the natural, not on the physical, but the spiritual. To run this race, we need the power of faith through the Spirit. Do not attempt this race without being reborn from above, you will fail. Moreover, do not attempt to be a spectator sitting in the stands and confess to be a Christian. The enemy will feast upon you; convince you that there is nothing for you to do for God, no divine purpose for your life and then your faith will fade; the fire of God's love will slowly go out and will only spark for a few moments on Sundays. God has called everyone to a task of faith in acts of mercy. A spectator can never know the true joy of victory, but only the one who is running in the race. Adam, Eve, and everyone else who has lived here except for One have all lost the race because of sin. However, Jesus Christ ran the race and overcame the obstacle of our sin. Christ has already won the victory over sin and settled the sin issue at the cross, but we need to know how to run in His victory, in His mercy and therefore, it becomes our victory.

Faith in Christ, which is always victorious, is rooted in every believer the moment we accept the sacrifice of Jesus Christ, but it must be developed, nurtured and tested. Faith, which is given by God through the Holy Spirit, gives all believers the power to become marathon runners for Christ.

What is faith? Faith is not just some positive thinking, or some mind over matter theory that the enemy has sown into the hearts of humanity. Faith is not trusting in humanity or in one's self-ability through reasoning and logic. God defines faith very clearly as hearing, believing and obeying His word.

Then Jesus said to those Jews who believed Him, "If you abide in My word, you are My disciples indeed." John 8:31

If we believe and act on what God said, then we are living in victory by obeying the truth by faith. God has given us the ability, the power through His Spirit and His written word to choose good over evil, light over darkness, life over death. This requires some work, dedication, commitment and something that is very important in finishing the race, endurance. What is endurance? It is the power to endure, the power to undergo, the power to move forward. Endurance is God's power to overcome every obstacle that is set against the knowledge of God. And God has given us that power by His Spirit, which is a witness in our hearts.

Therefore, I run thus: Not with uncertainty.
I will run the course of Your commandments...
1ˢᵗ Corinthians 9:26, Psalm 119:32

A True Friend

"...But I have called you friends."
John 15: 15

In an age of name-dropping, and the phrase 'it's not what you know, but who you know', becomes more dominant in government, business, and even in some churches, Jesus gives us a word that is worth more than our earthly connections. The word *friend* gives us a clear insight of how Jesus sees us, and cares for us, even if we cannot really comprehend it now. A *friend* is defined as a comrade, a partner and a companion, not just a connection. It is easy to understand why the lesser would want to be friends with the greater, but here we are, specks of dust, created from the soil of the earth, and then there is God; glorious, eternal, almighty, all knowing and all-powerful, and God calls us a friend. We see Jesus, who is the Eternal Son of God, in that all things were created through Him, and He calls us friends. Again, I can understand why the servant would want to be friends with the King, but why would the King what to be friends with the servant? The reason is simple, one we often overlook in our theology. It is called love, which is not always logical, not often predictable, and many times ignored. Nevertheless, *God is Love*, and that is why He loves us, because He is love, and not because of the specks of dirt that we are. God knows every detail about us, every sin and every evil thought, and yet He loves all those who trust Him by faith, even as a friend.

James tells us that Abraham was *a friend of God*, and John warns us about becoming *a friend of the world*. Therefore, we can clearly see that we have only two choices of friends, God, or the world. The *world,* as described in the Scriptures is man's system of operation, which is based on sin, because without God, sin is all we know. Yes, I know that this might be a profound statement to *the world*, however, according to God's word, and not the opinion of men, our nature is that of a rebellious, sin infected heart that makes us run away from God and hide, just as Adam and Eve did when they had sinned. The Scriptures are full of choices given to men, but every choice is either right or left, good or evil, love or hate, giving or taking, life or death, and it all stems from being a *friend of God*, or a *friend of sin.*

Why was Abraham called a friend of God? Abraham believed God, he trusted God at His word. Are you saying that the only requirement to be a friend of God is to trust Him? Yes, and God calls it faith. God has chosen the avenue of faith to redeem us from our sin nature by the power of the sacrifice of His Son Jesus Christ. Moreover, it is total trust in Jesus Christ, which is the faith that assures us an eternal pardon from the judgment of sin. The Scriptures tell us that *without faith, it is impossible to please God.* Faith is the thread that binds us together in spirit, and intertwines us with the Spirit of God. Without it, we are separated from the truth of God, blinded from the light of His love, and consistently looking for something to fill the void of an empty heart that only God can fill.

This I know, because God is for me.
Psalm 56: 9

Like a true friend, God is on our side. Like a loving parent, God is looking to protect us, and like the all-powerful King of kings, God rules over our enemies. That is right, God rules, and even if our circumstances might present themselves in that our enemies appear to be in control, do not buy it! God allows things to happen, but is always in total control. There is nothing that happens apart from God's knowledge that is, or will take place in all creation. Although we might not have the answers to why some things take place, we have faith, knowing that *God is for us*, and not against us. Therefore, even when evil turns its ugly face at us, by faith in Christ, we are not moved, because we have a friend in God, and His name is Jesus. Maybe not a friend in the front office or a friend that works in a high-ranking government seat. Maybe we do not know the mayor, the governor, or even a senator, but if you know Jesus Christ as your Lord and Savior, then you have an eternal friend who will never leave you, or forsake you.

A man who has friends must himself be friendly, but there is a friend who sticks closer than a brother.
Proverbs 19: 24

Trust Him

For this is good and acceptable in the sight of God our Savior, who desires all men to be saved and to come to the knowledge of the truth.

1st Timothy 2: 3

It is no mystery, there is no hidden meaning in the truth when God declares to us that His desire is for all people, young and old, black, white, red or yellow, rich or poor, educated or not, to come to the redeeming power of His love in Jesus Christ. For it is not through the means of merit, but by the free gift of grace. For God in His divine wisdom has chosen the path of faith in which we can be declared not guilty, receiving a full pardon for every trespass committed against God through the sacrifice of Jesus Christ, who was, is and always will be God the Son.

Why through faith? The real meaning of faith is trust, because without trust, real love cannot exist. I know that some might have different opinions on the true meaning of love, but God not only wrote the book on the subject, we are told in the Scriptures that *God is love.* Therefore, we exist because of His love, and for no other reason. We were not born in this life just because of a heated moment of passion. God is the Author of all life, and without Him, no one lives!

On the subject of trust, there is a story of a mountain climber who set out to conquer a very high mount. It was something he had accomplished many times before, trusting only in his own talents, and rejecting even the idea of God. Since many former climbing partners disappointed him, he now climbed alone. After many hours of climbing, a thick fog began to cover the mountain as the sun quickly vanished behind the earth and a deep cold began to set in. It was dark, so dark that the climber could no longer move on. As he attempted to rest from the climb, his foot slipped and he began to fall. As he was falling, he called out to God, and said, "Help me Lord'! Just then, the safety belt that was attached to a rope must have caught a tree limb, so there he hung, suspended between heaven and earth. He called out to God again and said, "Lord God, if you can save me from this, I will believe that you are and will follow you the rest of my life." Just then, a voice came from heaven and

8

said, "Do you trust Me?" The climber replied, "Yes Lord, I do." The voice from heaven said, "Cut the rope." The climber replied, "But I will die if I cut the rope, it is the only thing that is preventing me from falling." The voice from heaven answered, "If you truly trust Me, you will cut the rope." The climber could not bring himself to cut the rope, so he waited. After a few days had passed, a rescue team began to search for the man, and not many days later, found him frozen to death, with his hands clenching the rope. The rescue team was puzzled as they cut him down and asked one another,"Why didn't he just cut the rope?" For his frozen corpse was only three feet from the ground.

If any man or woman desires to be saved, they must cut the rope of self-security and begin to trust God without doubts. If we continue to hang on in only trusting ourselves instead of placing our faith in the one and only Christ, then we also will die with a frozen heart, only to discover later that we were so close, that we were only a prayer away from eternity.

"For the Son of Man (Jesus), *did not come to destroy men's lives, but to save them."*

Luke 9: 56

We might trust our doctors, our accountants, our financial advisor's, even our lawyers, only heaven knows why we would do that, but we are hesitant to trust God with not only our many problems that we face day after day, but even with our eternities. Some might rationalize that they cannot trust somebody they cannot see. However, God tells us that faith is *the confidence of things unseen.* We cannot see gravity, yet we know that it is. We cannot see the very air that we inhale; yet, we know that it exists. We see the effects of gravity and oxygen but the substance we cannot. Much like God, the effects, the reflection of His love is evident in all that He made, that includes us. If we can trust, or have faith that we will breath oxygen, and know that when we wake in the morning our feet will hit the ground, why should we not trust God that He loves us by the evidence of the reflection of creation? God does love us, so much that He sent His Son, Jesus the Christ from the throne of heaven to earth to become a one-time sacrifice for every sin we have committed against God. This is the truth, the only answer, and the only cure for the eternal terminal spiritual illness called sin. We also hang from a rope of uncertainty if we have not received the very sacrifice of Christ into our hearts. It is a rope of doubt and hopelessness that will surely bring us all to the darkness of judgment. However, if we are willing to cut that rope, the rope that ties us to the shame and slavery of sin, by calling out to the name, which is above every name that is given to man, through the name of Jesus Christ, by the power of His sacrifice, we are redeemed. No longer hanging in the dead zone of unbelief, but standing on the solid rock foundation of Jesus Christ, trusting in His faithfulness, His love, and His sacrifice of mercy.

For by one offering He (Jesus Christ) *has perfected forever those who are being sanctified.*
Hebrews 10: 14
We are then set free from the ropes of the imaginations of rebellious men that create their own theologies, excluding the One and only true God and making themselves their own god. For the ropes of these fabricated, synthetic theories are without an eternal hope, without forgiveness, they are without love. They are simply a poor attempt to justify their own sin, and they themselves are choked by the weight of shame. There is no peace offered in the empty religion of man's philosophy, because there is still the guilt of sin and a bondage to it. As the climber who had found himself in the darkness of a fallen nature, and was unable to save himself because of darkness, we also, unless we conclude that God is our Savior, are doomed to face the tragedy of judgment for the error of sin. Without trusting in God's redeeming quality of love that was displayed before men and angels on two pieces of wood, there is no hope, because every man and woman that has ever existed has fallen short by sin, and unable to reach a perfect, holy, and righteous God. God could never just ignore sin, but paid for it Himself, leaving us a way of escaping the judgment of Hell.

To Our Leaders

For with what judgment you judge, you will be judged...
Matthew 7: 2

While our media continues to magnify issues such as raising the minimum wage, increased taxes and higher fuel cost, the defining of moral foundational truths, the building blocks of a society with good conscience, that have stabilized this nation throughout our every battle, has been laid on the wayside and trampled under the feet of sold out politicians and poorly appointed judges. Either the real issues that will shape the future of the next generation of Americans are ignored, or sugar coated with neutral opinions that are based on position insecurities. While some who do not have children, may not be concerned of what kind of mess we leave behind, those of us that do have offspring, hope that we can contribute something more than a crumbling moral society that has altered the true meaning of liberty and justice. We are infected from within the boundaries of our own democracy with a misconception of how to define the precious gift of freedom that was paid for by the blood of men and women that were willing to sacrifice all for truth, justice and the American way of life, which are words that rarely share a headline in today's news coverage. This gift of freedom, that is now prostituted with words like 'the right to choose', was not conceived or birth in the mind or heart of any man, but mandated by God right from the beginning, giving the first couple freedom to choose what is good over evil, and leaving them responsible with full accountability concerning their choice. In today's democracy, we see an attempt to abide in freedom without accountability, which is communicated through the opinions of conscious numb leaders that are more interested in political gain, rather than assuming responsibility for the moral teaching of the next generation, and have already handed over supreme authority to state judges who are assuming an almighty position of ruling according to their own ideas. It is impossible to maintain a working union of justice based on human ideas and opinions that can easily differ from person to person and from generation to generation. For if, we are unwilling to recognize God as the Judge of all judges, the ultimate, supreme authority of our frail human makeup, and then it is simply like asking a four year old to babysit for another four year old. Without a reverence to a higher authority, then the ruling class assumes the role of playing god, which will result in a decay of a decent, moral society. Moreover, it is in the classrooms where the decay will begin, and has already begun, and will surface twenty or thirty years later as young minds are influenced by a weak government that no longer abides in the confines of morality, and continually redefines the Constitution, and the very source of that document, the Bible. If we continue as a nation in rulings based on opinions and ideas, rather than the solid foundation of God's undisputed truth, then we will lose the effectiveness of a ruling body that is united in cause and purpose. We are already witnessing a society that no longer abides in the truths of life, but is confused in the consistent changes of opinions, which teach our young that life is not a precious gift, but rather is something that can be aborted, like a cancelled dinner party in the name of 'Pro-Choice.' These are only the beginnings of a grumbling foundation, as even marriage is redefined by opinions, and let us not even mention divorce, which has already been accepted as an aborted oath of trust. We could spend hours on each of these gross errors. The very structure of a man and women in a consecrated union before God has been reduced to the perversion of those who practice unlawful acts in leadership. Look at the evidence of such errors, it is in the headlines everyday as we see drug abuse, murder, greed, and perversion fill our prisons to over capacity levels. History has shown us repeatedly that these rebellions against the laws of truth will leave any nation in a decay of ruin. Have we not learned anything from the errors of times past?

Leaving the Ten Commandments out of the building structure of the next generation is like building a house without the support of beams. The house might look good with all the trimmings and final touching of detailed artisanship, but with the first strong wind of opposition, the house will go down, leveled to dust. This country was founded, nurtured, and protected by the moral reference to God's mandates through leaders that understood the importance of a solid framework that will build a society of law abiding, mature adults that know and understand the value of God's intervention regarding our safety and our standard of true justice in a country that is free from the dictatorship of any one man, or woman that places themselves above the law of God. There is no middle ground, no luke-warm opinions, no liking the left, but leaning to the right. There is a line in the sand that marks whether we are going to stand on the solid foundation of God's mandates of true justice, or sink in the quicksand of the perverted opinions of shortsighted officials that would rather be served, instead of serving by the very oath they confessed before men and God. Consider the tides of error that are drifting our true sense of freedom out to a sea of lost nations. Consider the enormous consequences of those nations that are now lying on the ocean's floor of defeat and shame, that were unable to return to the shore of God's truth, but are now destined for a judgment that far outweighs any man made court. Please consider your votes on every key issue that sets itself against a much higher ruling than those of men, and vote for those laws that will build a strong foundation of morality for the next generation, so they might reap the blessings of victory, instead of the curses of defeat. For any nation that is not protected by God, is simply not protected. May God have mercy on us?

Unless the Lord of Host had left us a seed, we would have become like Sodom, and we would have been made like Gomorrah. Romans 9: 29

Every believer in Christ is the seed of morality, the seed of His truth and the seed of His love. We need to make that seed known to the leaders of this nation, or else face the future of a faithless generation.

In Jesus

*"Then Jesus cried out and said, "He who believes in Me,
believes not in Me, but in Him who sent Me."
Jesus said to her, "I am the resurrection and the life, he who
believes in Me, though he may die, he shall live."
And Jesus said to him, "I am the way the truth and the life, no
one comes to the Father except through Me."
John 12: 44, 11: 26, 14: 6*

While some made-man religions preach justification through
works, call on the name of saints, and some call on Old
Testament names that described the nature of God, Jesus tells
us very clearly that He alone holds our redemption and our
avenue to divinity. Moreover, there is no other way to obtain
eternal life except through Him. Jesus could not have made it
clearer when He declares the truth that any other way that man
might attempt to redeem himself from the gross error of sin will
simply lead to a dead end, a literal spiritual dead-ending of life,
which the Scriptures define as separation from the Creator.
Jesus did not come to start another religion so man can justify
himself by attending a weekly service, which will by no means
cover the debt of sin. After all, while the Christian church has
been divided by theological disagreements, the true religion
should have been Judaism, since it is the basic core of faith in
Christ, but under a New Covenant of redemption. We now
believe what Judaism has rejected. Not to get side tracked in
these divisions, or the many false teachings that are present in
the misinterpretation of Scripture, but Jesus taught that it is by
Him alone that we may know the truth (in a relationship with
Him), and that we may have a resurrection to eternal life with
God. We can call out to the name of saints until we are blue in
the face. We can call on the Old Covenant names given to God
in attempting to express His greatness from morning into the
night. We can practice every good work, feed the poor, deny
every pleasure, and sacrifice even our own blood, but without
faith in Jesus Christ, it is all in vain. For without Christ, all things
that might bring applause of merit from men are still stained
with sin. Have you ever tried to remove a grease stain from a

pure white garment? You can bleach that garment until the threads are breaking apart, but that stain will remain. Jesus testifies that without Him, the stain of our sin remains, because we could not pay the price for our sin, we do not possess the purity that is required, it is simply beyond out reach, but Jesus did.

...Who gave Himself for our sins, that He might deliver us from this present evil age, according to the will of God the Father... Galatians 1:4

The Gospel of Jesus Christ is a simple message of the grace of God, that by His desire, sent His Son as an eternal blood sacrifice for the forgiveness of sins for all that believe through repentance. For Christ is our only advocator! An attempt to justify ourselves to the only all knowing, all righteous, absolute holy God, with sin stained hands is not even thinkable, since if our sin remains with us, so does our guilt and shame. For God knows all, He knows every single detail of our lives. But the greatest news that rings through the galaxies is that in spite of our sin, God loves us, so much so, that He was willing to save us from the eternal consequences of sin by sending His Son to pay the price for our every trespass against righteousness. How much easier could God have made it for us? Before Jesus inhaled His last breath on the cross, He declared, *"It is finished."* All the work for the redemption of man was completed that day on the cross, leaving no unfinished work. The truth of our forgiveness lives in Christ, because not only did He die for our sins, but He also was raised from the dead for our eternity. Jesus Christ now lives, representing us in a living trust, by the power of a New Covenant, purchased by the cost of His blood.

For the love of Christ compels us, because we judge thus: that if One died for all, then all died, that those who live should live no longer for themselves, but for Him who died for them and rose again.

For He made Him who knew no sin to be sin for us, that we might become the righteousness of God in Him.
2nd Corinthians 5:14,15,21

God is in Control

Therefore humble yourselves under the mighty hand of God, that He may exalt you in due time, casting all your cares upon Him, for He cares for you.
1st Peter 5: 5
In a world that is filled with backbiting, gossip, conceit, slander, selfish motives, hatefulness and resentment, God assures us that He is surely big enough to deal with any evil that has spoken its ugly tongue against good. Peter, through the power of the Holy Spirit tells us, instead of allowing our pride to lash back at the tongues of evil (that are nothing more than the fiery arrows of demons), trust God by humbling ourselves to His mighty hand. Is it easy to turn the cheek? No! Is it easy to remember that God is the Judge of all judges, and He alone will judge every evil act? No! However, God tells us that we must for several reasons.

- The first and foremost reason is that if these evil acts of deceit are delivered by unbelievers, then we should surely have pity on them, for they are headed for an eternity of suffering and pain unless they turn to Christ.
- The second is that we need to remember that just as God uses people to spread the Gospel, the devil uses people to stop it. The saddest part about those who are used by Satan is they have no idea that they are being used and abused by the very one who would like to kill all of us at 6:00 in the morning. Unbelievers do not realize that Satan hates them just as much as he hates believers.
- The third and most important thing we must remember is that God *cares for us.* That statement means that God is concerned and is already involved with every aspect of our lives. God tells us to humble ourselves to His power, and He will deal with all those who set themselves against His people. Anyone that has set their minds against the people of God has set their hearts against God directly.

...And be clothed with humility...
God resists the proud, but gives grace to the humble.
1st Peter 5: 5 & 6

How many times does God have to tell us the same thing? Of course, our biggest problem is that we want God to react in our timetable. However, God is God, and He knows the best time to deliver, or to judge. Who knows, it could just be that by our humble reaction to evil that is spoken against good, a soul might be saved from an eternity of judgment. Who are we to place ourselves in the position of God and curse someone to everlasting punishment because our feelings might have gotten hurt? We need to remember that God is the Judge of all judges.

Bless those who persecute you: bless and do not curse.
Do not be overcome by evil, but overcome evil with good.
Romans 12: 14 & 21

This is the true fruit of the Spirit, that although some might obey the voice of evil, as we all have done at some time or another, we that now believe have the confident, assured hope that love is stronger then hate, and good will always overcome evil. It is easy to lash back at the voices of ignorance, those who are perishing from a rebellious heart. However, the true evidence that the Holy Spirit abides in the heart of a believer is the power to *overcome evil with good.* This is the outward manifestation of God that declares to those who are drowning in a sea of sin that God still loves them. Anyone that has fallen in the pit of deception is already living in a hell that is filled with resentment, hurt and the inability to forgive. This condition is like a cancer that slowly eats the heart of anyone that yields to that call.
In the words of the Master Himself:

"But I say to you, love your enemies, bless those who curse you, do good to those who hate you, pray for those who spitefully use you and persecute, that you may be sons (and daughters)*, of your Father in heaven; for He makes His sun rise on the evil and the good, and sends His rain on the just and the unjust."*
Matthew 5: 44 & 45

This is by far the biggest challenge, the greatest lesson, and the hardest concept to follow of all the teachings of Christ. Yet, Jesus reassures us that God Himself is kind and merciful to the ungrateful. Yes, God loves those who rebel against Him. All those that use His name in vain, those who curse Him and blame Him for all their errors, God still allows them to enjoy His blessings of creation, but only for a limited time. Therefore, who are we to judge and condemn the lost? For all judgment belongs to the Lord. Therefore, we can stand in the light of faith in God, knowing the He is in complete control.

"Let your light so shine before men, that they may see your good works and glorify your Father in heaven."
Matthew 5: 16

Repay no one evil for evil. Beloved, do not avenge yourselves, but rather give place to wrath; for it is written, "Vengeance is Mine, says the Lord, I will repay," says the Lord.
Romans 12: 17, 19,

For we know Him who said, "It is mine to avenge; I will repay, "and again, "The Lord will judge His people." It is a dreadful thing to fall into the hands of the living Lord.
Hebrews 10: 30-31

Nevertheless, God's hand of mercy is always open to anyone who is willing to humble himself or herself, repent and return to His love.

Seek the Lord while He may be found, call upon Him while He is near. Isaiah 55: 6

Let all bitterness, and wrath, and anger, and clamor, and evil speaking, be put away from you, with all malice: And be kind to one another, tenderhearted, forgiving one another, even as God for Christ's sake has forgiven you.
Ephesians 4: 31,32

Follow peace with all men, and holiness, without which no man shall see the Lord: Looking diligently lest any man fall short of the grace of God: lest any root of bitterness springing up trouble you, and thereby many are defiled.
Hebrews 12: 14,15

Giving Thanks

…With thanksgiving, let your request be made known to God…
Philippians 4: 6

I know this might sound like a Thanksgiving Day message, but if we know the faithfulness of God, then every day is a day of thanksgiving. Yes, I know that some might say, 'Here comes another one of those optimistic idiots that thinks life is a bowl of cherries.' Trust me; I know firsthand that life can be tough. I also know that those who drown themselves in a sea of negativity will find themselves in a state of defeat, missing the true purpose of life. For no one can be a victim and be victorious at the same time. There are many times in our journey when we hear a moving story that affects us for a few hours, even a day. It makes us think how wonderful our lives are, and then we quickly forget. This is what happened to the Israelites when God delivered them from the hands of an evil empire. They quickly forgot the supernatural exit from Egypt and saw only a desert of despair. As the Israelites did in the desert, we also lose sight of how blessed we really are, even forgetting that our very existence is a supernatural act of God. The above text tells us to make our request known to God with *thanksgiving.* I recently heard a story from a man who was involved in a terrible accident. He told me that one day he had a flat tire while driving home from work. No doubt, this was a typical day in the life of this man. He pulled over and went to his trunk to get out the jack and spare tire. The next thing he remembers is lying on a windshield of a car while his legs were pinned against his rear bumper and another car. It was a drunk driver that slammed into him on the side of the road, leaving both legs crushed. When they arrived at the hospital, it did not take the doctors very long to notify him that both legs had to come off. He told me that he pleaded with the doctors to try to save at least one leg, the doctors agreed with very little hope. Both legs were hanging on by a thread. Now this man could have easily become bitter, questioning God as to why this had happened to him. But instead, he hoped that at least one leg might be saved, and it was. So, instead of being confined to a wheelchair, today this man walks with one artificial leg, and even more than just walking, he works as a limo driver, providing for the needs of his family. Is this man thankful that he only has one leg? He will tell you "yes." I know we have heard all the common phrases like, 'It could be worse', or, 'There is a silver lining in every cloud.' However, stories like this are a wake-up call for all of us that find ourselves drifting into the sea of negativity. It is easy to be negative, to criticize everything and everybody that does not match our way of thinking. However, the true victory over negativity, which is like a cancer that eats away at any hope that is within out spirits, is in the understanding that all things here are temporal. Our time here is short, and our moment of departure is unknown. We need to remember that the evil in the present age might be able to take away some things, or even some people that we cherish, but as long as there is hope in God, there is an expectation that can fill our hearts and minds with the strength to move on. The real issue is that without faith in God, we have no hope. Moreover, hopelessness gives birth to bitterness and resentfulness. I believe that God sends us people, not always behind a pulpit, and not always someone with a degree in theology, but rather people that might have suffered a great physical loss, but their faith in God was untouched, and can still look up to the throne of grace and say, "Thank you." For it is in the thankful and grateful heart where God hears our prayers and will answer them, maybe not always in the time and fashion according to our limited understanding, but according to His endless love.

Be thankful...
Colossians 3: 14

The Darkest Night

And being in agony, He prayed more earnestly. Then sweat became like great drops of blood falling down to the ground. Luke 22:44

It is only in the figment of our imaginations that we might capture the darkest night of all nights since the creation of man. Although Adam and Eve certainly closed the window of heaven, boarding it up with the betrayal of sin, even on that night there was a small glimmer of light from God. However, on the night that Jesus was betrayed there was a darkness that was void of any light, a cold blackness of judgment that was reserved for the sins of men. I believe that if it is possible for God the Father to cry, this might have been the night that a tear was shed down His face. We might have read this story repeatedly, to the point that we become numb to the full impact of the words written. However, the above Scripture tells us that *great drops of blood* were falling from the face of Jesus. Scientists have concluded that it is possible to sweat blood due to an enormously high level of pressure (blood pressure), due to great stress placed on the mind and body. Anyone who has experienced the symptoms caused by severe high blood pressure will testify of a massive headache, feeling like their head is ready to explode. Moreover, as the pain increases, so does the heart rate, beating frantically. Even that severe state of stress is shy to the point of sweating blood. Therefore, the amount of pressure that was on Jesus that night is beyond our comprehension. The sufferings of Jesus due to the weight of our sin were not merely physical, but mentally as well. This statement is not meant to downplay the physical beating that Jesus experienced, but rather to show that the mental suffering for our sin was just as severe as the brutality to His body. The reason is that none of us, no not even the worst murderer we could think of, ever experienced the total absences of God's light of love, and the blackness of God's judgment while still in these mortal bodies.

…He makes His sun rise on the evil and the good, and sends rain on the just and the unjust. Matthew 5: 45

However, on the night that Jesus entered a covenant with God the Father, offering Himself as the final blood sacrifice for the forgiveness of our sins, the *blackness of darkness* fell on the mind and Spirit of Christ. Hours before He would lay Himself on the altar of the cross, the shame and anguish of every sin committed by every person born into this world fell on Him. The weight of man's curse could never be carried by someone who himself had sin. That would be like cleaning a grease stain with a greasy rag, all you would do is just spread the grease. Moreover, just as we cannot imagine being totally absent from the light of God's love, neither could Jesus predict the pain of total separation from the Father. As the darkness of God's judgment began to fall on Him, and Jesus began to taste the cup of God's wrath, His blood begins to rush in His head, His heart begins to race like a locomotive engine; He sweats blood, mixed with tears. Moreover, even in that incomprehensible anguish, Jesus submits Himself to the desire of the Father, knowing that through His sacrifice, we would be granted the eternal pardon for all sin, the sin of every man and woman. And without it, we will experience this awful judgment.

But God demonstrates His own love toward us, in that while we were still sinners, Christ died for us.

Much more then, having now been justified by His blood, we shall be saved from the wrath through Him.

...Much more, having been reconciled, we shall be saved by His life.

Romans 5: 8 - 10

Worth much more than any riches, pleasures, or an achievement in this life is the eternal life, paid for by the *great drops of blood* that was shed by the King of all life.

Risen Sunday

"He is not here, for He is risen as He said."
Matthew 28:6
Have we heard the story of the risen Christ so many times, that maybe we have become numb to the reality of what took place? Do we hear the words of the woman who ran back to the disciples rejoicing with tears of joy, *"He is risen?"* Have we forgotten the pure joy of knowing that because He lives, we have eternal life? Do we find more excitement in other pleasures than in the celebration of the risen Lord? Are television programs or sports events more thrilling than the worship to our Savior? Have we turned our hearts cold to the greatest news that has ever been given to humanity because we are busy with the daily responsibilities of this life? For one day, we will leave here and stand before the throne of God, so why not re-evaluate our priorities and give some thought to these questions now.
The first reaction of His closest friends was that somebody stole His corpse. Yet, we read repeatedly how Jesus foretold the event of the cross and how He would rise on the third day. All His disciples and all the people whom He healed, including Mary did not hear His words, *"On the third day, I will rise."*
Many religions portray Jesus hanging dead on the cross and their services are like a funeral that mourns His death. That does not make much sense, since Jesus is alive, not dead! Why would we mourn His death when we can celebrate His resurrection? These empty religions are like themselves, a corpse, dead to the Holy Spirit, unplugged, disconnected from the very source of all life.
But the angel answered and said to the woman, "Do not be afraid, for I know that you seek Jesus who was crucified. He is not here, for He is risen…" Matthew 28:5, 6
Do we go through the robotic rituals of a Sunday service and in all the time in God's presence we are thinking of somewhere else that we would rather be? Is it just out of obligation that we fulfill our religious duties? Have we made a wrong turn somewhere on the road to God?

I would not spend my time or money in a church that has forgotten how to worship God. We are not going to a tomb where a dead corpse lay as a piece of stone, but we come to a living Christ, whom death could not hold. Mary and all the disciples where told repeatedly by Jesus Himself, *"On the third day I will rise."* I find it so strange how not one of them believed it, even after some of them witnessed Jesus raising the dead.

When Jesus raised Lazarus from the dead, his sister came to him crying, and Jesus said to her:

… *"Your brother will rise again." Martha said to Him, "I know that he will rise again in the resurrection at the last day." Jesus said to her, "I am the resurrection and the life."*
John 11:23 – 25

Jesus was not just a life; He is the Author of Life, the very power that causes our hearts to beat. He was not just resurrected; He is the resurrection, the very force of God that gives renewed life. The awesome power of all life is in Jesus Christ. Yet some of us go to a dead church, sit in a dead service for one or two hours, listen to dead words, and walk out feeling just as dead as when we walked in. It is not a question of denomination; it is a matter of whether we are spending our time in front of an empty tomb or in front of the living Christ. Mary, Martha and all the disciples of Jesus did not get it when Jesus said, *"On the third day I will rise."* I wonder if we really get it since it does not seem to be a reality in most churches. Jesus said something very important to Martha when the subject of life came up.

"He who believes in Me, though he may die, he shall live. And whoever lives and believes in Me shall never die. Do you believe this?"
John 11:25, 26

Jesus said, *"he who believes, whoever lives and believes in Me."* That *"he* and *whoever"* is talking about you and me. If we really believe in Jesus, believe He died for our sins and He was raised up on the third day from the dead, then Jesus is talking about us! Not that Jesus was only talking to Martha, Mary, Peter or John. This is something to celebrate in worship everyday that we wake up and open our eyes. Jesus asked

Martha the most important question in the entire universe; *"Do you believe this?"* This question is for each one of us. It is a timeless question, which holds the key for eternity. We all are being asked this question everyday, because our eternal destiny is depending on it. The choice is ours! The question is requiring a yes or no answer. It is either left or right, darkness or light, believe or a believe-not question. There are no shades of gray in the answer to this question. Do you believe that Jesus is who He says He is? Do you believe what the reports (the Scriptures) say about His life, His death and His resurrection from the dead? If our answers are yes, then we have eternal life by faith in Christ. Therefore, it should never be an obligation in going to any church that worships Christ. When Mary realized that she had not come to a tomb where a dead body lay, but to a risen living Jesus, she could only do one thing, she worshipped Him!

So they came and held Him by the feet and worshipped Him. When they saw Him, they worshipped Him…
Matthew 28: 9 & 17

For I delivered to you first of all that which I also received: that Christ died for our sins according to the Scriptures, and was buried, and that He rose again on the third day according to the Scriptures, and that He was seen by Cephas, then the twelve. After that, He was seen by over five hundred brethren at once, of whom the greater remain to present. But some have fallen asleep. After that He was seen by James, and then by all the apostles. Last of all He was seen by me also, as by one born out of time.
Romans 15: 4 – 8

Jesus lives! Make no mistake about it, Jesus is alive and all those that believe in Him will live with Him for eternity.

Ants

Go to the ant, you sluggard! Consider her ways and be wise.
Proverbs 6: 6
God tells us to *consider,* observe the ant, whom some might perceive as an insignificant little creature that has nothing to teach us. However, there is something to learn when we watch these insects carry out their daily task with precision and harmony. Each one has a job to do as they assemble, working for a common objective. There is no fighting, no backbiting and no resentments, because none of them labor for their own good, but for the common good of all. They understand the true meaning of teamwork. And if one falls, the other will carry him if need be. Moreover, since they are united in purpose, they are not intimidated by the size of any task. They can do so much damage to a house that is 100,000 times their size because they work together for the same goal, all aiming for the same target. This bond of unity causes the ant to be a force of strength. Moreover, the ant is continually preparing for the good of the next generation, building colonies with an inter-structure of devotion and sacrifice toward one another, fully understanding their purpose. Maybe this is where some of the confusion has made camp in our hearts and minds, being fully convinced that the purpose of our lives is in self-pleasure and self-contentment. We have all been deceived by the lie that 'you only go around once, and then that is it.' However, the truth of the matter is that this life compared to the endless span of eternity, is like a single thread that is sown in a blanket. Every great man and women of faith that has been recorded in the Scriptures understood that they were just passing through this life for a brief moment in time, but were preparing for the after life where time has no place. They also understood that the gift of this life that was granted by the Creator of all life was not just to fulfill their own desires, but to fulfill a divine plan of love and purpose.
The ant's knowledge in the true meaning of unselfish giving to preserve their lifeline is staggering. There is no greed in these little creatures, no gluttonous behaviors, no wanting it all for myself attitude. The ant goes through a short, and what would

appear as an insignificant life span, barely noticed by those around them until they make their presence known by a pressing forward into our living space, always with a purpose in unity. The ant has discovered the gem of all diamonds, the riches of all wealth, because they live in a purpose of unselfish order. There is no greater wealth, no higher achievements, or no greater satisfaction than knowing the true purpose of living. Moreover, since we are given the gift of life, we are accountable to the One who gave it, to use it for His intended purpose. Although this fact continually evades us, one day, which could very well be tomorrow, all of us will have a day of accountability. Yes, I know that this is a subject that none of us wants to think about. However, in any event, it will happen, not to some, but to all of us.

Although some might say that the ant is unable to reason, yet without a degree in theology or physiology, they have abided in the most rewarding aspect of life. They are willing to give of themselves for the cause of another, which is the true, pure definition of love. Yes, I know that Hollywood magnifies the human depravity of lust and defines it as love. However, true love was magnified in the birth, death and resurrection of Jesus Christ, who gave His all for our sake. He forsook Himself, willing to pay the price of death that we may have life.

God tells us to consider, watch, and observe the ant as they work in the true meaning of life. It is no wonder why God calls the ant wise, and yet so often in the Scriptures He calls man a fool!

Understand you senseless among the people; and you fools, when will you be wise?
Psalm 94: 8

What's Next?

The way of righteousness is life, and in its pathway, there is no death. Proverbs 13:28

Have you ever wondered about what happens next? I mean after our lives have finished the course of these brief moments in time. How often have we seen a loved one, or someone we might have known suddenly pass away? One minute they were there and the next minute they were gone, just like that. Not to dwell on the departing of a loved one, but just think for one moment how the time goes by. The years are rolling faster and faster. And one day it will be our turn, then what? Some people might think that the body is all there is and we simply don not exist when the body ceases to function. So what is the purpose of our existence? Is it just to live for a short time and then die? That is a sad and empty thought. But let me share with you what God says about this subject, since God is the Creator and Author of all life and He knows what He is talking about when we read His word on life and death. In the above verse, God makes it very clear that there is an eternal path of life; it is a path that has no end. And since God alone is righteous, then the way of God is life. Therefore, if we are grafted in with Him in spirit, then we are on the path of life. Not that anyone could boast of self-righteousness, but if we are united with His Spirit, then we are also united in His righteousness, which is life. And on God's pathway, there is no death. Yes, our bodies will fail, but our spirits will be released and soar like an eagle, because our spirits live on. There is no reason to fear this separation of body and spirit once on the path of life. The path goes on and on, never ending.

I will ransom them from the power of the grave; I will redeem them from death. Where, O death, are you plagues? Where, O grave is your destruction? Hosea 13:14

The ransom has been paid with the blood of the Son of God, Jesus Christ! Those who believe on the Son are redeemed from the grip of the second death, which is clearly defined in the Scriptures as total separation from God, forever! However, this death has no sting, no power, and no hold on all that have accepted the sacrifice of Jesus Christ. It was for this very purpose that He came. Yes, our bodies will give out one day, but life is in our spirits. Like an egg, that once you have cracked opened the shell and the egg white and yoke are then separated from the shell, the shell is discarded, but the yoke and egg white are used. Our bodies are only a shell to house our spirits. Without the spirit, our bodies cease to function.

So, as the body without the spirit is dead... James 2: 26

God makes this very clear, stating that we have a physical body and we have a spirit. There should be no question marks on this issue; God could not say it any clearer. The natural body will die, but the spirit is eternal. If we have established this fact, then the next question is, so where does my spirit go? The word of God tells us the only two options we have. God teaches us about His path, the path of righteousness, His righteousness, not ours. And if we choose to walk down the path of God, that He has paid for and purchased for us, it leads to eternal life in the presence of the Almighty. But if we choose our own path without the mercy and forgiving grace of God, then our spirits are in a place of eternal separation from God, which the Scriptures call a living hell. This is much worse than any non-existences state that we can imagine. Throughout the word of God, the two paths are mentioned many times. God gives us a choice, left or right, His way or our way, life or death. Why should we walk on God's path? Because God paid for that path by the blood of His Son, it is the only way that we can be forgiven for our sins. Jesus said, *"I am the way, the truth and the life, no one comes to the Father except through Me."* Jesus is the only way to God, the only way to redemption, the only way to eternal life. Do not be fooled by empty theologies, or swallow physiology. Faith in Jesus Christ is the only *way*, the only *truth*, and the only eternal *life*.

My Peace

"Peace I leave you. My peace I give you; not as the world gives do I give you."
The Prince of Peace...
John 14:27, Isaiah 9:6

In a world of marketing and advertising that attempts to sell the most desirable product, making claims to fulfill our inner thirst for contentment with all the trimmings, falls far short when it comes to peace of the soul. This is not to deny that all the high tech., newly designed, fashionable, sleek and comfortable things that tickle our eyes do give us some short-lived pleasure, until something newer, bigger, or more exciting comes along. However, even during this short period of contentment, do we have peace? It is something we cannot purchase; is it wrapped in a box, labeled and marketed with a limited warranty? Is it obtained through catalogs, online shopping or in the local department store? In the above Scripture, Jesus tells us about His peace, a peace that not all the riches in the world could ever buy. Is this just a peace of mind that Jesus is promising, or a peace deposited in our spirits by God that brings our minds and hearts in the understanding of His love toward us? There is a peace in knowing the ultimate security of God's passion and commitment to rescue us from an eternity of error, which is freely given, not earned, or purchased with material wealth. Even in our deepest relationships, as in the covenant of marriage, there can be an absence of peace. The true inner peace of God, which comforts our troubled minds, can only come through the *Prince of Peace* Himself, since Jesus Christ is the one who holds our eternity in His nail scarred hands. Some might gain financial security, and security in a loving spouse and family. However, the peace that Jesus speaks of is from within, and not based on external conditions or circumstances. It is not through the canal of material possessions, academic achievements, or titles. True peace is not from a carnal security, but from a spiritual birth. We have seen many people that possessed all that the marketing campaigns had to offer, only to see them in a cell of bondage to a never-ending discontentment. I know in my own life, no matter what I possess, no matter what goal was achieved, no matter what new hobby I invested my time in, I was never content.

With a life of pleasure, material wealth, and having anything that his heart desired, the wise King Solomon says, *"Vanity, vanity, all is vanity."* All the riches, all the pleasures, all the so-called power that most people eagerly run after, are all empty, vain, unfulfilling efforts without the peace of God. They are all mere temporary substitutes for the real, everlasting peace and contentment of mind and spirit that can only be received from Jesus Christ Himself. Yes, I know that some might put on a smile, laugh and parade around as to say, 'look at me, I have it all.' However, without the peace of assurance, all the rest amounts to zero, nothing, it is a dead end.

After a life of gratifying his carnality, and realizing that it will never fill our inner need to be united with the Creator of all life, Solomon gives the final words of wisdom.

"Fear God and keep His commandments, for this is man's all. For God will bring every work into judgment, including every secret thing, whether good or evil."
Ecclesiastics 12:13 & 14

The peace of God, which is given by faith in Christ, is the result of a pure conscience toward God, no longer chained by the shackles of guilt and shame. It is the understanding that Jesus has truly paid our debt of sin in full, no balance due. Therefore, it is His holiness that has swallowed up our sin. His obedience that has cleansed our disobedience, it is His faithfulness that has erased our unfaithfulness, and it is His act of mercy that has redeemed us for eternity.

For He (Christ), *Himself is our peace.*
And the peace of God, which surpasses all understanding, will guard your hearts and minds through Christ Jesus
Ephesians 2: 14, Philippians 4: 7

More than a Sparrow

"Are not two sparrows sold for a copper coin? And not one of them falls to the ground apart from your Father's will. But the very hairs of your head are numbered. Do not fear therefore, you are of more value than many sparrows.
Matthew 10: 29 – 31

We live in a society that has reduced the value of human life to the mere opinions of leaders with no conscience in the name of freedom, which is only a disguise for the true motive of selfishness. This might offend some that hide behind a mask of hypocrisy, and even distort this nation's declaration of human rights. However, Jesus pulled no punches. He does not attempt to be politically correct when He teaches us that the life of a bird, or any other created thing, has a far lower value compared to the worth of a human life. Jesus tells us that *the very hairs of your head are numbered,* meaning that God knows and observes even the smallest detail in our lives. Even more than that, this statement clearly tells us how much God cares for us. Now some might ask the faithless question, 'If God loves us so much, why do we see such an abundance of evil in the world today?'

We all have freedom of choice. God has given us the freedom to choose good over evil, truth over a lie, and life over death. We have the power to tell a lie, or tell the truth, to steal or to give, to kill or to save. Those who point the finger at God are ignorant to even their own identity and concerning the power of choice that they possess, attempting to blame even God for their own errors. However, in all of this mess, above all the corruption, murder, deceit and selfishness that abides in the heart of man, there is a way to truth, peace, and life eternal. Can we say that ten sparrows are worth as much as the life of child? Are twenty sparrows worth more that a man or a woman? Can one hundred or maybe one thousand of any creatures equal one human life? I think not! We could stack sparrows upon sparrows until they filled the entire universe, and they would never be equivalent to one human being, because we are speaking about a much higher order of life.

However, if there were a human being, which somehow could become a sparrow (without ceasing to be a human being), we would have a sparrow that was worth more then every bird that ever existed. This is the heart, the center of the message concerning God's love for us.

...Jesus Christ, who, being in the form of God, did not consider it robbery to be equal with God, but made Himself of no reputation, taking the form of a bondservant, and coming in the likeness of men.
Philippians 2: 6 & 7

Above every philosophy, every theology, and every man made religious myth, the truth of the Gospel of Jesus Christ is alone the only floodlight of hope in the darken nights of our fallen hearts. God the Son became one of us, because there was no other sacrifice for sin that was pure enough to cancel the debt of error, which is the death of judgment. God became a man:

...The Word was God. And the Word became flesh and dwelt among us...
John 1: 1, 1: 14

This is why John the apostle opens his gospel with the truth of identifying the deity of Christ as God the Son before he begins to testify of the things he had seen and heard.

What is that you say? You don't buy into it? It does not take a rocket scientist to observe how short this life is. For at any given moment this life could end for any of us, regardless of race, creed, or even age, the death of these bodies awaits us all. However, the only missing piece is that we do not know when, but death will surely come. Compared to the timeless span of eternity, this life is but a glance of a moment. So, what is next? The Bible tells us repeatedly that there are only two places, two very different destinations in that we will live forever. God provided a way, not many ways, but one way, through one sacrifice, to spend eternity in His presence with no guilt or shame from sin. Jesus became our substitute for the judgment of our every transgression; therefore, He is the only way.

"For God so loved the world (humanity, even in the present condition of human affairs, alienated from God), *that He gave His only begotten Son, that **whomever believes in Him** should not perish but **have everlasting life.***"
John 3:16
God did not *so love* the sparrow, the whale, the lion, or the eagle *that He gave His only begotten Son.* God so loved us, since we were created in *His image and likeness*, unlike any other living thing, even the angels. The Scripture says; *"Whomever believes in Him"*, not whatever believes in Him, for God gave His Son for us. How much more does God have to prove to us that He loves us? Moreover, the only requirement for the promise of eternal life is faith, since God Himself tells us *"That whoever believes in Him* {Jesus), *should not perish but have everlasting life.* Much more than the sparrow, God values us, and desires to spend eternity with us. This is not to say that the animal kingdom or even the earth has no value, but certainly not the value of a human life. For humanity is a higher order of life, with a living spirit. Although man failed and slipped into the sea of transgression, God's love provides a life raft, a life preserver for all that are willing to come to the grace that God has freely given. All the mercies of God are in Jesus Christ.
For all have sinned and fall short of the glory of God...
But the free gift is not like the offense....
Romans 3: 23, 5: 15
For God sent not His Son into the world to condemn the world; but that the world through Him might be saved.
John 3:17
Neither is there salvation in any other: for there is no other name under heaven given among men, where by we must be saved.
Acts 4:12

34

Eternal Life

.... That you may know that you have eternal life... John 5:13
What is all this talk about eternal life? I mean we are all going
to die. And who wants to think about death anyway? And how
can anyone be sure that he or she is going to live forever? All
valid questions and all have answers. I know most people's
opinions are, let me live today, and tomorrow, who knows? I
have heard this statement so many times from all types of
people. Let us live for today. However, just think for one
moment. What if you did have a spirit and this spirit did not die?
What if by some chance, this spirit, which is something you
cannot see, is very real? What if this Man Jesus, who is a
historical fact, is whom He says He is? This question needs to
be settled in our hearts and minds, so we can move from doubt
to faith in God.
Moreover, truth can be proven in any courtroom by the
testimony of noble eyewitnesses. The Apostle John writes an
account of events into a testimony as an eyewitness.
*This is the disciple who testifies to these things and who wrote
them down.*
John 21: 24
The Apostle Peter writes an eyewitness account of what he
heard and saw.
*We ourselves heard this voice that came from heaven when we
were with Him on the sacred mountain. 2ⁿᵈ Peter 1: 18*
In addition, the Apostle Paul, who was an enemy of all who
believed in Jesus gives His eyewitness account.
*...That Christ died for our sins according to the Scriptures, and
He was buried, that He was raised on the third day according to
the Scriptures, and that He appeared to Peter, and then to the
twelve. After that, He appeared to more than five hundred of
the brothers at the same time, most of whom are still living,
though some have fallen asleep. So then He appeared to
James, and then to all the apostles, and last of all He appeared
to me also, as to one abnormally born.*
1ˢᵗ Corinthians 15:3
So, let us look at these three testimonies. All three are stating
in writing that they are eyewitnesses. All three men testify as

eyewitnesses, they were there. John says that he testifies to everything that was written about Jesus. Peter says that he was an eyewitness when a voice came down from heaven to Jesus. In addition, Paul testifies, not only did over five hundred people testify to seeing the risen Jesus at once, but that Jesus also appeared to him.

Were these men looking for fame, money or attention? Well two of these men died for what they believed, that does not sound like fame to me. The other man was exiled on an island. Everything else in these men's' lives seemed very small compared to the gift of eternal life. The treasure of knowing God changed their lives. Paul who was in tune with the Spirit of God writes this:

But when God, who set me apart from birth and called me by His grace was pleased to reveal His Son to me...
Galatians 1:1

God was and is willing to reveal His Son, Jesus Christ to you and I. For every minute that Jesus lived here in the flesh, God was revealing Himself to us.

Who being in the form of God did not consider equality with God something to be grasped.
Philippians 2:6

God does not need a testimony, God does not need a witness, God does not need anything, He is over all creation.

Nevertheless, God is willing to express His love for us through His Son, Jesus Christ.

And this is the testimony: God has given us eternal life, and this life is in His Son. He who has the Son has life; he who does not have the Son of God does not have life.
1ˢᵗ John 5:11

Forget Not

"Beware that you do not forget the Lord your God by not keeping His commandments, and His statutes which I command you today."
"If you love me, keep my commandments."
Deuteronomy 8: 11, John 14: 15

God teaches us the basics of faith, loyalty and devotion, to direct our paths of understanding toward His heart and the hearts of each other. The message is clear and simple as God instructs us that if we love Him, we will do what He asks, knowing that His directive is always for our best interest. The above Scriptures reveal the real meaning of love, for if we truly love someone, we do not easily forget about them and discard whatever they ask of us. Moreover, if we truly confess to love God, then His commands are not burdensome, but a privilege that is followed with honor and respect.

For he who lacks these things is shortsighted, even to blindness, and has forgotten that he was cleansed from his old sins. 2nd Peter 1: 9

It is easy to forget times, dates, places and even people that we have encountered in this short earthly experience. For some, even family members can drift so far apart from us that they are on the borderline of forgotten. However, as Peter writes these words by the power of the Holy Spirit to the church, not to unbelievers, but to believers, he explains that we need to remember all that the Lord God has done for us. This is something that the Israelites had a hard time with, as they soon forgot the exit from Egypt. Therefore, forgetting God, they were stuck in what seemed to be an endless circle of doubt, which gave birth to complaining, depression and uncertainty, which is what we hear from most people everyday. Have you ever felt that way? Maybe that is because we quickly forget that God has delivered us, cleansed us from our past and will deliver us again through every storm of this life if we are only willing to listen to Him. Remember that God loves us and is only interested for our good. He knows what is best for us and wants us to grow in His love.

The Lord is my shepherd...

"I am the good shepherd. The good shepherd gives His life for the sheep."
"I am the good shepherd; and I know my sheep, and am known by My own."
Psalm 23: 1, John 10: 11, 14
It might hurt our egos that the Lord Jesus refers to us as sheep, which are defenseless, with no natural weapons of protection, and certainly not one of the smartest animals in creation. Sheep are so dumb that if one runs off a cliff, the rest will follow. However, at least they know their shepherd, and the sound of their shepherd's voice; they understand that the shepherd protects them from the wolf. Therefore, although we might be compared to as sheep, at least we can know the Creator Himself as our Shepherd who loves us and guides us in the green pastures of His peace, security and His strength. This might be a thought that we can easily forget in the times of hardship, or times of pleasure, but the Lord tells us, *"Beware that you do not forget the Lord your God...."*
In the remembrance of His love is power over every circumstance that attempts to prevent us from keeping His commandments. The results of being mindful of His promises will be God's strength in us, which is victorious over evil, instead of being victims of evil.
...And when the Chief Shepherd appears, you will receive the crown of glory that does not fade away.
The Lord is my shepherd, I shall not lack, he makes me lie down in green pastures; He leads me beside the still waters, He restores my soul, He leads me in the paths of righteousness for His name's sake.
1ˢᵗ Peter 5: 4, Psalm 23: 1 - 3

Got Faith ?

So Jesus said to them, "Because of your unbelief (lack of faith)*;
For assuredly I say to you, if you had faith as a mustard seed,
you would say to this mountain, 'Move from here to there,' and
it will move; and nothing will be impossible for you."
Matthew 17: 20*

Our doctors tell us to exercise our bodies daily, even without
question we all know that a regular routine of exercise will
strengthen our immune system as well as our supporting
framework, being knitted together with muscle. The teachers
tell us to exercise our minds daily with reading comprehension,
communication and even troubleshooting problems that
sharpens our thinking. All these things are good within
themselves; however, God tells us that the most important
exercise we can perform is to exercise our faith in Him.
Moreover, God will give us the opportunity for a good spiritual
workout, using real life problems to stretch our spiritual
muscles, so to strengthen our spiritual frame in trusting Him
more every day.

In the above text, Jesus gives us a lot of information about faith
in a rather short statement. Prior to this statement, His disciples
had attempted to vacate an evil spirit from a young boy without
any success. They came to Jesus and asked Him what the
problem was. If I may paraphrase His response, Jesus,
basically said; 'If you guys had just a tiny, little bit of faith, even
smaller than a mustard seed, not only would evil spirits obey
you, but any other mountain that is a resistance to God in your
lives would also have to vacate the premises.' That statement
is a hard one to swallow, since most of us have trouble with a
little bump in the road, no less a huge mountain in our way. We
need to remember, without faith in God, nothing will move out
of our way, which tells me that for most of us, our faith is even
smaller than a mustard seed. So how do we grow in faith?

Everyone that exercises their physical bodies does it for a
reason, a goal, an objective, whether it is to regain a good
health status, or lose those unwanted pounds, or both. The
main point being made here is that there is a reason to start
this physical routine of sweat and sacrifice to achieve an

objective, whatever that objective may be. This is true for every goal in our lives, whether it be for our careers, or for our hobbies. It is no different with the exercise of faith, because faith in God brings forth results. We might not always be able to see the final destination of our destiny, but God knows and sees the place where He wants us to finish the course in faith. Therefore, if we want to move the mountains of roadblocks in our lives, we need strong, big faith.

Anybody that has begun a physical exercise program will tell you without hesitation that getting started is the hardest part. Vision is needed to start any program. Without a vision of a goal, there can be no motivation, since we need to visualize the results, or to say it another way, have an idea where we are going to end up. Some people that begin a dedicated commitment of exercise and a diet program will place an old picture of themselves or a picture of someone that they admire on their refrigerator to remind them of their objective before they open the fridge and start eating something that is not inline with their diet. They set their minds on the objective with a constant reminder of their prize.

Set your mind on things above, not on things on the earth.
Colossians 3: 2

Comparing this with the discipline of faith, it is so important to read the word of God daily, since it is like that picture on the refrigerator that reminds us daily of our goal, which is to reflect Jesus Christ in our lives everyday and soon to be with Him for eternity. The vision of faith is in the word of God, which will produce motivation, dedication and the restoration of our spirits. The promises of God give us a reason to exercise our faith, seeing how God worked with people throughout the Scriptures. I have never met anyone that was engaged in a disciplined physical exercise program that was performing a routine workout for no reason. We are purpose driven spirits, which explains why so many people fall into deep depression when they lose their purpose for living. No vision results in no motivation, no purpose, and no victory.

However, once a vision of understanding is revealed, it gives birth to motivation, and then comes the desire to become disciplined or a disciple to the desire, which will also mean some sacrifices will have to take place, as in making time for God.

Now look again at faith through the same view as someone that begins a dedicated, committed physical exercise program.

- Vision is no doubt the first step in beginning a serious faith exercise program. Without it, we stumble in the darkness of ignorance, walking in circles, much like the band of stiff necked people that God had so graciously released from the bondage of Egypt. Because of their lack of vision, around and around they went, never entering God's destiny for their lives, circling in the darkness of their own error. Now true vision comes from God, since He is the Truth, God alone can open our spiritual eyes for His plan for our lives, through His word. Maybe not the whole plan, but enough to get us started in faith.
- Planning is the second step in beginning any type of exercise program. Although we do not totally know the future, we can plan a consistent spiritual nutrition program, preparing us for faith building test by reading God's word, for *faith comes by hearing the word of God.* Therefore, once we have faith, after being born in the kingdom of God through Jesus Christ, we can then build faith muscles through a steady diet of God's word and faith experiences that align with God's word. It only makes sense that before anyone can travel to a destination, a finish place of traveling, there must be a planned objective. There is no difference with career goals, family planning, diet objectives and even pleasure activities than with planning spiritual growth through faith exercising. Now every student that is engaged in a steady learning process, which in fact we all are, whether it is a believer or an unbeliever, will encounter tests to assure that the material that was studied has been absorbed in our minds. Again, there is no difference with faith, only that the Teacher who

administrates the test in faith is the one and only God. For just as faith is tested, so is our love for Him and each other, in an effort to help us realize the true important things in this short experience on this earth. *For by it* (faith*), the elders obtained a good testimony.* *Hebrews 11: 2*

From Abraham through John the Baptist, there was a testimony, an outward confession of faith as many declared the promises and the warnings of God to rebellious generations. Abraham was so persuaded by the command of God that he moved from his hometown, changed his name from Abram to Abraham, and above all, was ready to give his only son as a sacrifice. Noah also was ready and willing to abandon all his selfish ambitions and followed God's command to build a boat, designed to go nowhere. The list can go on and on, as men and women declared a confession of faith*, a good testimony* with their mouths, and with their actions. Not with their mouths only, but their actions followed their declaration that God is faithful to accomplish all that He had said. All of them were ready to leave behind their own dreams and ambitions and lay aside their own agenda to please God. Of course, God always exceeded any dream or hope that they might have had, and can do the same for us. They all accomplished tasks of faith, through faith in God, and the exercising of faith through actions and not by word alone! Paul goes on to preach that the Israelites also pursued God through actions, the righteousness of the law, but not by faith, but through obligation. *But Israel pursuing the law of righteousness, has not obtained to the law of righteousness. Why? Because they did not seek it by faith.* *Romans 9: 31 & 33*

Therefore, just as *faith without works is dead,* so works without faith is also dead. For faith is the only requirement for salvation, since all redemption was already completed on the cross as Jesus declared, *"It is finished."* However, to walk in that salvation and to come into a deeper relationship with God, faith is required, mandated, commanded, because we cannot please God apart from faith in Him. We cannot confuse works of faith as a merit for salvation, but rather because someone is saved from eternal damnation, faith is birthed and matured. If we cannot believe God for the smaller things in life, what will happen when the mountains of trouble confront us? It is as if asking someone who never physically exercises to run a marathon.

When the storm came upon the boat while Jesus was fast asleep and His disciples were drowning in their own fear, Jesus asked, *"Where is your faith?"* For in the absence of faith, fear will build a house, however, in the presence of faith, fear will vanish. Faith is the vehicle that God has chosen to bring us through this life and into His eternal presence. Faith is simply trusting God for our every breath and every heartbeat, and most of all, for our eternities.

If any of you lacks wisdom, let him ask of God...
But let him ask in faith, without doubting, for he who doubts is like a wave of the sea driven and tossed by the wind. For let not that man receive anything from the Lord; he is a double-minded man, unstable in all his ways.
James 1: 5 – 8
He replied, "I tell you the truth, if you have faith....
Nothing will be impossible for you."
Matthew 17: 20

Surrender

Your will be done...
Matthew 6:1

Surrender is a word with echoes of defeat attached to it. It is a word that describes shame and weakness, or to simply give up. The word itself insults our pride; it shames our image of ourselves. It is a word that mocks us. All of these terms apply to the surrender of the strength and will of our minds. All are in the natural, given to the natural reaction of our insecure makeup. However, there is more to us than just flesh, bones and blood. There is also a spirit, which is the true heart, the center of our being. Though for the moment it may be unseen, it is the inner part of our makeup, the life source of living.

It is our unseen spiritual nature where real love exists, because real love is conceived, birth and lives through our spirits and not simply through carnal attraction. The spirit does not come from the reproduction between a man and a woman. God gives the spirit, just as there are created celestial beings that God created, made of only spirit and no outer shell of flesh, so man also is a spirit being with a shell of flesh.

"It is the Spirit who gives life; the flesh profits nothing..."
John 6: 63

In our natural, the word surrender insults us, sends a defensive rush of blood through our every vein because it signifies the giving up of our individuality, thinking that if we ever really surrendered to God in submission to His word, we would miss all the fun, and end up being a monk somewhere in the mountains of Italy. However, in the spirit, which is the very core of our life, surrender to the will of God is by far the greatest victory in the entire universe. We are not talking about the surrender to an empty religious philosophy, but the submission to love in a relationship with God the Creator of all life.

We are all so accustomed to living according to our own rules that are derived from personal experiences, that we lose sight of the big picture. The big picture is that God loves us and wants to protect us, even from ourselves at times and is not looking to rob anyone of his or her individuality, God made us, each one of us unique, different from anyone else. It is an interesting thought that nobody is like you, with the same fingerprints, the same DNA, and another you never existed before, and will never exist again. That is what I call true individuality according to God's will and not our own. God is not looking for robotic, look alike clones, but He made us different from one another according to His will. Therefore, the surrender in submission to God is by no means the losing of our individuality, or personality, but the entering into an eternal relationship with the Creator of all life in obedience to His will. After all, He is God. He has all power to give life or to take it away. We should be obedient to His will since He has granted us life by His love. Moreover, it is eternal life that we are speaking of when we enter into a relationship with God where there is no time, which our minds cannot grasp now. A relationship with God requires submission to His will, since He is all knowing, which means that there is nothing that God does not know about the past, the present and the future. Without submission to God, we simply make ourselves our own god, which is a delusion, deceiving ourselves in thinking that we have some kind of immortality without the Creator of all life. Now faith is birth in trusting God at His word and knowing that God knows what is best for us, like a good parent that tries to warn their child of the dangers of evil. I hope that you can see that God is not looking to take away our lives, but rather give us an abundant, eternal life in His love. And the only way to enter in His love is to accept His plan of salvation, which is far better than any plan we could ever come up with on our own. By trusting God at His word, we can discover how much God really does love us. God could have easily made us robotic puppets, but instead, He gave us the freedom of choice between good and evil, life and death.

Not everyone who says to Me, 'Lord, Lord,' shall enter the Kingdom of Heaven, but he who does the will of My Father in Heaven.
Matthew 7:21

Jesus gives us a clear view of what God commands of us. God is looking for us to surrender in submission, agree to His will, like a good child who submits to the will of a wise and loving parent. Let us then clarify what being in the will of God defines. God allowed us to be here, present in this certain time. God is not a dictator who wants to boss us around. We need to always view God as the loving Father that He is, but God also rules and is the Judge of all judges. God has given us free choice and does not dictate our every action. However, God has a temporary and eternal purpose for every one of us. There are no accidental births. God called us into existence for a purpose, since God has a purpose for everything that He does! Do not be fooled into thinking that we are here simply because of human will. God alone is the Giver and Sustainer of all life! Without God, we are simply without life.

The word of the Lord came to me, saying, "Before I formed you in the womb I knew you. Before you were born I set you apart."
Jeremiah 1:4 – 5

Notice how God takes full responsibility for creating us. He told Jeremiah, *"I formed you in the womb."* God, the Creator of all life, certainly does the work in the womb of any mother, there should be no question about this; God calls us into being. God also told the prophet, *"Before the womb, I knew you."* God is not bound by the restrictions of time; He sees the future as if it is the past.

Now we have our free choice, because God wants us to submit to His purpose willingly and not begrudgingly.

Isaiah received the same revelation as Jeremiah:
And now the Lord said, "He who formed me in the womb to be His servant to bring Jacob back to them and gather Israel to Himself."
Isaiah 49:5

Now you might say, 'Don't I have a choice of my purpose in life?' We do have choices in this life, and God expects us to make good choices, to choose good over evil, but there are only two choices for eternity! Our destiny is in our own choices. God's way is the best choice we could ever make. Our way, just look at the world today, corrupted in so many ways. The earth itself has been abused, and the world, man's system stinks of murder, corruption, lying, injustice and greed. All of us have been taught that money is what defines success; we have all been a victim to this line of thinking. There is nothing wrong with money, but the problem begins when we worship it. When we begin to believe that money is the answer to all our problems and when we begin to devote ourselves to money instead of God. We have all seen many wealthy and famous people die alone, broken hearted, confused, bitter and dependant on substance abuse. The current condition of the world is a reflection on how man has drifted further and further away from the Creator. On and on we go, the earth turns another day and we think to ourselves, things are not that bad, as the world falls deeper in sin. However, God tells us that in times past, there were societies so deep in sin, refusing to submit to God's holy purpose that God executed swift judgment. Jesus uses these two moments in history to show us a glimpse of where man is currently heading.

As it was in the days of Noah, so it will be at the coming of the Son of Man.

It was the same in the days of Lot. People were eating and drinking, buying and selling, planting and building. But the day Lot left Sodom, fire and sulfur rained down from Heaven and destroyed them all.

Matthew 24:37, Luke 17:28 and 29

Two moments in time when only two men *(Noah and Lot),* knew enough to surrender in submission to God. Two men who made an intelligent decision to turn their backs to sin and their faces toward the Creator. Jesus uses these two men and their moments in time as an example of how man will continue to fall in error unless he turns to God. I am sure those societies viewed these men as foolish, weak, and not in touch with reality. Nevertheless, Noah and Lot knew the greatest victory that anyone could possibly experience. They knew to surrender, listen and obey God. These two men, who believed and trusted God, were brought to safety before His wrath was delivered.

Is there victory without God? Is there freedom without God? Silly questions! Throughout the Scriptures, we see men and women as examples. Some of them submitted to God and some did not. In each instance, we can see that God always wins and those who submit to His word will walk in His victory. We can also read about those who refused God and found themselves defeated in every sense of the word.

These are not just bedtime stories, but living examples. We are not talking about some fables, or some myths. God's word stands by the power of the Creator, undisputed, without controversy, it is the whole truth and nothing but the truth. However, without the true act of surrender in submission, the truth will escape us. We will only catch a glimpse of it from the corner of our eyes. Then, when we turn our heads to look for it, it is gone!

"Lord, if it is you" Peter replied, "Tell me to come to you on the water."
Matthew 14:28

I saw a book that was titled, If You Want to Walk on the Water, You Have to Get Out of the Boat. If we can go to the movie house of our minds and rewind this scene of Jesus walking on the water. The Scriptures tell us that when the disciples saw Jesus walking on the water, they were terrified. I can picture some of the disciples. Some who were big fishermen, who fought with the sea, wind and rain all their lives, doing the back step in the boat. Have you ever been terrified? I mean these guys were scared! These guys would have crawled into the wood of the boat if they could have found a place to hide. Chances are the disciples were so scared they could not move. In any event, the Scriptures tell us that they cried out in fear. Peter, who the rest of them were probably hiding behind, steps up to the plate. I am sure his knees were shaking, but Peter had some faith. Peter says to Jesus, *"Tell me to come to you on the water."* We all know that walking on water is not natural. Our minds reject the very thought of such an act. However, Peter had courage, because it takes courage to take the first step of faith out of the natural and into the supernatural power of God. To submit our lives to the will and purpose of God is the most important step of faith we will ever take and does take courage.

God revealed to the Apostle Paul that once our faith is strengthened with solid spiritual legs, we will run the race of faith! That is where God wants us to be. He wants us to grow up in faith so we can run instead of taking a step, then stumbling and falling. It all begins with an act of faith called surrender in submission to God's will.

There are times when our problems surround us like the wind that frightened Peter. We take one step toward God, and then we fall because we doubt His word, just as Peter fell when he looked down and saw the raging sea. But God tells us that we can run the course of faith even on the water, but it takes hearing, believing and submitting to His promise. Our problems can overcome our thoughts as the wind overcame Peter. When that happened to Peter, he began to sink, and then he prays the shortest prayer in the Scriptures, a prayer we have all prayed many times, *"Lord save me."* Peter had no time to start a study on Old Testament prayer that day. Those three simple words reached the ear of Jesus and the Scriptures tell us that immediately Jesus reached out His hand and caught him. I would say that Peter prayed an effective prayer. Jesus did that for Peter, he will also do it for us, if we call on Him in faith. Jesus asked Peter the same questions He will ask us every time we begin to fall or sink, '*You of little faith, why did you doubt?'* Why do we doubt God? If we know how powerful God is, if we know that He loves us with an eternal love, then why do we have such little faith. The answer is because we have not completely surrendered in submission to His word. The true act of surrender is confessing with word and deed that we trust God unconditionally in total submission, which is our greatest victory!

Love Heals

And above all things have fervent love for one another, for love will cover a multitude of sins.
1ˢᵗ Peter 4:8

Many people go through this life with scars in their hearts, (an emotional bruise) that never heals. The deep cut could have happened years ago or just the other day, nevertheless, it happened and at the time that it happened, it hurt. For the pains of the heart are the worse pains known to us. They can leave us with a hard, callused heart, a heart that is unforgiving. Some people are too proud to admit a hurt so they just carry it around throughout their entire lives, wondering why they are never at peace. The hurts of the heart will turn to thorns of bitterness. In the Gospel of Matthew, Jesus tells us the story of how a certain king forgave the debt of a servant. The servant, who was forgiven by the king of what he owed, would not forgive the debt of someone who owed him much less then he owed the king. When the king found out about it, he then asked the servant this question:

Should you not also have had compassion on your fellow servant, just as I had pity on you? Matthew 18:33

This important question should be answered by each and every one of us. Let us re-phrase the question to mean the same thing but in different words. If God has forgiven you, should you forgive others? Now the result of not forgiving someone is sin, and that lack of forgiveness will leave a cut in our hearts that will remain open and bleeding. The hurt will then begin to build a protective wall around our hearts to protect our feelings, and this can leave us cold hearted and insensitive to the truth of how to love. The state of this heart that is in an unforgiving mode is a heart with no peace. I know many people who smile and laugh on the outside, but on the inside their hearts are bleeding, because of bitterness and resentment. This is why God wants us to forgive one another. Not forgiving one another does more damage to us than to anyone else; it is like a cancer that eats us from the inside. Forgiveness is for our own benefit. God knows what He is talking about when He commands us to forgive. He knows that forgiveness heals the hurt, it removes bitterness and resentment, and forgiving is the most powerful way of showing the ability to love. We know that real love, based on unselfishness, is the most powerful force in our lives. *God is love.* Moreover, one thing that can prevent us from forgiving is our pride, and God tells us that a proud heart is a foolish heart. A forgiving heart, is a wise heart and can heal the wounds from the past or present. There are no other options, there is no other way but by love. This type of love is the very nature of God. I have heard people say that they want to get close to God, to understand Him, to worship Him. However, how can you do that without the power of loving forgiveness in your heart? Love conquers all, even unforgiving! Nothing can stand against love! Love is given from God, since it is a part of His very nature. God's love is expressed in and through the life, death, and resurrection of His Son, Jesus Christ.

For God so loved the world that He gave His only begotten Son...

...And every one who loves is born of God and knows God.

...Whoever believes that Jesus is the Christ is born of God. 1st John 3: 16, John 4:7, 5:1

Forgiveness is the by-product of love. Without love we cannot forgive or give of ourselves. When we allow God to work His power of love in us, if we are willing to yield to His instructions, then a process will begin to expose and heal the scars or open wounds of our hearts. Without God, without His Spirit, who leads us into the courts of His presence, it is impossible to know true love. God is the source of love and without the source, there simply is no power. True love will always lead us to a deeper truth of Jesus Christ. Don't miss your chance to allow the power of God's love to work in your life. Forgiveness is the key that unlocks the door to peace with you, peace with others and peace with God. Moreover, in the peace of God, we will know the truth and the truth will set us free from any hurts from the past.

...That we may know Him who is true; and we are in Him who is true...

1st John 5:20.

God is Good

"But as for you, you meant evil against me; but God meant it for good…
" Genesis 50: 20

As the Holy Spirit finishes the book of Genesis through Moses, we see Joseph make such a statement of truth that will ring throughout the entire bible. God gives us a great example through the life of Joseph of how evil will set itself against those who love God. We all know the story, how Joseph was a victim of jealous brothers, sold into slavery, and then imprisoned by the wife of his master, accusing him of rape, again being a victim. Have you ever been in a place when things looked bad, and then they just get worse? Have you ever been an innocent victim before? If we could chart the life of Joseph, we would see a high peak of living in the first fifteen years of his life, then suddenly a straight downward line heading for the bottom of the page. It was as if Joseph was pushed out an airplane at sixty thousand feet, and was free falling into a fatal end. Joseph was no doubt a victim of evil, but not in his heart. Yes, on the outward appearance of circumstances, Joseph was a victim, but in his heart, he was victorious. Joseph learned the most valuable lesson in all of life while in the pit, while a slave, and even while in prison. Yes, I know we can read about the life of Joseph, and view it as a simple bedtime story with a happy ending, but his story is packed with life changing wisdom concerning the heart of God. Joseph discovered the truth of real faith, and not the kind of faith that is only strong when all is well. The faith that Joseph displayed was unshaken, uncompromising, but most of all, forgiving. This kind of faith, which is given by God, should prove to us without a shadow of doubt that if we do not let evil conquer our hearts with unbelief, no matter what circumstances we might be in, *all things* will *work together for good.*

And we know that all things work together for good to those who love God, to those who are the called according to His purpose.
Romans 8: 28

The hidden key to God's heart is that if we trust Him, which is faith, and do not doubt His timing, although some might intend to do evil to us, God will turn it in to good, because God is by our side as long as we stay on His side.

This I know, because God is for me.
Yet in all things we are more than conquerors through Him who loved us.
Psalm 56: 9, Romans 8: 37

No matter where we might be in this life, no matter how many times we have been let down, no matter what setbacks we have experienced, God is above them all. God is stronger then our worst failures, He is more powerful then our pain, He is more faithful then anyone we will ever know. God is for us, and if He is for us, who can be against us? As Joseph was pushed into a pit, sold out by his own family members, made a slave and then dragged off to prison and through all that, Joseph knew that God was for him. Every other human being that was around Joseph might have been against him, but Joseph never stopped believing God. He never became bitter, never resentful, but always hopeful, because his hope in God was the one thing that could not be taken away. He was forsaken from every direction, but he was never forsaken, or forgotten by God. Moreover, if God did it for Joseph, He will do it for us. Although the roads might get long, and the nights might become dark, God is watching and guiding those that trust Him. I am sure that if Joseph could sum up his life experiences in a few words he would say that even as a slave or in a prison cell, God is still faithful, and God is always good.
Whenever I am afraid, I will trust in You. In God(I will praise His word). In God I have put my trust; I will not fear.
What can flesh do to me?
Psalm 56: 2,3

The Gates

"Enter by the narrow gate; for wide is the gate and broad is the way that leads to destruction, and there are many who go in by it. Because narrow is the gate and difficult is the way which leads to life, and there are few who find it." Matthew 7: 13 & 14
The Sermon on the Mount has to be by far the most powerful and the most revealing character of God that has ever been taught to humanity. Jesus delivers this message with the intentions of clarifying the position of God's heart toward our lives. These chapters are full of the black and white distinctions between good and evil, and rewards verses judgment. They can bring the light of God's wisdom and love into our thinking pattern, and will change our lives and the lives of those around us, if we are willing to walk in them. The words of Christ are as a massive floodlight in the dead of night, like the ones used by emergency crews that shine on automobile wrecks, so the workers can see the hurt victims. For through our experiences we will encounter many lives that are wrecked from decisions made in ignorance because of the darkness of sin. This single sermon can give us the truth of right and wrong, not in our own opinion, but in God's command.

When taking one sliver of truth from this life-changing sermon, we can conclude to several facts that should clearly affect our daily lives.

Narrow and difficult is the way which leads to life. God clearly speaks of only two ways in which a person can go into eternity. Satan has really confused this issue with all the different so-called faiths, leaving most people with the question, 'which one is the true faith?' This is a clever detour of the enemy to derail hearts in thinking that there are many ways that leads to the mercy of God. However, God speaks of two ways, one to life and the other to death. One way is *narrow, difficult* and will demand discipline in all we say and do. The other way is *broad*, meaning; go with the flow, the easy way. The easy way influences us to think that since everybody else goes there, or does that, it cannot be that bad as we reason to ourselves, after all, I am not a bad person. Again, Jesus speaks of only two ways that a person can travel through the journey of this life and into eternity. The things we say, the places we go and the things we do certainly determined the road we are on, because all these decisions are based on our thinking patterns that are either influenced by the word of God, or contrary to it. There is no deep hidden spiritual secret in this, what a man or woman thinks, he or she eventually does. For all actions begin with thoughts and it is in the mind where the choice of right or wrong, justice or injustice, good or evil, forgiveness or resentfulness, peace or war, love or hate, life or death, the narrow gate or the broad gate are all presented to our freewill. Even in a circumstance where someone is a victim of injustice through the ignorance and the blindness of hate, that one still has a choice to carry the heavy load of bitterness, or to forgive and move on to another day. These gates are before us every day, and although there may be many variables, we need to choose the right gate in our every thought. Is it easy to always choose the right gate? Discipline is never easy; ask anyone who has been on a serious diet. Discipline requires commitment and commitment requires a passion to whatever we commit ourselves. A person, who needs to lose weight, or stop smoking, drinking, lying, stealing, or the less obvious sins like gossiping or complaining, must have a passion to change, or change will never take place. Is it easy? Jesus said that the *narrow gate* is *difficult*. Change is hard, difficult and not something any of us find pleasurable. However, through the knowledge of Jesus Christ, a passion is birth within us to enter in that narrow gate with every decision in our daily lives. This lasting passion can only be born through the grace of God, and it is by His will, by the goodness of His mercy that we are able to understand anything that is holy. Moreover, through the understanding of the love of God in Christ, we are able to choose right over wrong, good over evil, even life over death. As any woman has the freewill to do whatever she wants with her unborn baby, God says, *"Choose life."* Yes, some choices are clearly harder than others are, but with the light of understanding, through the knowledge of Jesus Christ, we can choose the *narrow gate.*

God also gave Moses two choices to give to the people, in that he would present to the children of Israel, which coincide to the two gates that Jesus taught. *"Now it shall be, when the Lord your God has brought you into the land which you go to possess, that you shall put the blessing on Mount Gerzim and the curse on Mount Ebal. Deuteronomy 11: 29* Two mountains, as two gates, represent salvation or judgment, blessing or a curse, these are the two choices that are presented to us every day. Choose life, choose Jesus Christ, for today and for eternity, because our life here could end and our eternity could begin at any given moment. But for those that believe, we have an eternal house with God. *For we know that if our earthly house, this tent* (the physical body), *is destroyed, we have a building from God, a house not made with hands, eternal in the heavens.*
So we are always confident knowing that while we are at home in the body we are absent from the Lord. For we walk by faith, not by sight. We are confident, yes, well pleased rather to be absent from the body and to be present with the Lord.
2ⁿᵈ Corinthians 5: 1, 6 -8
For in the gift of our salvation, God rejoices and welcomes all who trust in Him with open arms and an open heart, because He cares for us and loves us with an eternal love that does not fade or wear out.
And as the bridegroom rejoices over the bride, so shall your God rejoice over you.
Isaiah 62: 5
"They shall be My people, and I will be their God; then I will give them one heart and one way, that they may fear Me forever, for the good of them and their children after them. And I will make an everlasting covenant with them, that they will not depart from Me. Yes, I will rejoice over them to do good...
Jeremiah 32: 38 - 41

CHANGE

...And be renewed in the spirit of your mind.
Ephesians 4: 23
How many of us would like to have our minds renewed, cleansed, washed from the garbage we see and hear on a daily basis? Even from the ignorance that comes out of the mouth of those that fill themselves with the cup of pride and from the actions of unhappy, unfulfilled people that continually attempts to grab pleasures and material possessions in a vain effort to satisfy their inner emptiness. These all affect our minds like someone throwing mud on the windshields of our cars and we then attempting to drive without rinsing it off. Moreover, let us not forget the world of advertising, the greedy kingdom of marketing, that some of them would prostitute their own sons and daughters for the sake of a major contract with a big name. We could go on and on about the corruption in the hearts of many businessmen as well as many political leaders who claim to represent the people, but are self motivated, even drunk for the thirst for more power. Does all of this have an effect on our minds? It does, and without the hope of being redeemed by the power of God, it is like a cancer that slowly eats away at us, leaving some with a soul filled with bitterness and resentment. Even with all the self-help books, all the teachers that preach a positive perspective will all admit that unless there is a renewing of thoughts, then nothing can change in a person's life.

For as he thinks in his heart, so he is
Proverbs 23:7
Without hope, without faith in the living God, these positive teachings are like someone standing in a filled cesspool and convincing themselves that I am going to look at the bright side. That might work for a little while, but in time, they will begin to complain, wanting a way out. And when no other way is found, then the answer will be something that can just simply take away the reality that I am sinking in a cesspool. The answer becomes numbness, with the reasoning that if I just ignore this mess, simply become numb to it all, it will not affect me, but it does! I have seen this everyday as I speak to people who are

angry, bitter, and without hope. However, those with hope, with faith in the one and only God, through Jesus Christ, can be cleansed, and removed from the cesspool of selfishness, and crowned with the eternal light of God's love, if we are willing to allow His word to cleanse our minds. There is a change that must take place, a change of heart and mind, which will also affect our thinking. That change of heart and mind can only come through the forgiveness of sin, which cleanses the spirit. Once that happens, then we need a daily cleansing from God's instructions. If anyone thinks that their mind can be cleansed without having the spirit cleansed first, they are deceiving themselves. It is a confession of faith in Jesus Christ, with a repenting heart that cleanses the spirit from all sin. However, even by the power of God, who alone can forgive all our sins and all our errors, we have the responsibility of rinsing our minds clean on a daily basis with the water of the word of God. Think of it as taking a daily spiritual shower to remove all the dirt that we see and hear from an unbelieving world. Once our spirits are redeemed, sanitized, sanctified, bleached clean by the faithful, sinless, holy blood of Christ that was shed for us by the mercy of God, only then can our minds be renewed by the power of God's word by reading it everyday. Our carnal minds are at war with our spirits. Therefore, a change of mind that is led by the Spirit of God is essential, so to avoid returning to the cesspool of sin. It is no mystery that while we are digesting a steady diet of God's word, little by little our minds are being washed from the ugly stain of sin that once dominated our thought patterns, because our spirits were dead. This does not happen overnight, but is a process that takes time. In many areas of my life, I could not see the change happening quick enough. I was still plagued by a quick temper, and quick to point the finger of judgment, among other things that hindered my walk with God, therefore, hindering my prayers. However, God is stronger than our minds, and if we continue in feeding our minds with His truth, change will come by His power. God brought me back to an early time in my life, a time when I was anxious for change, but the change was just taking too long for me. When I was young, much younger than today, I needed braces for my teeth. I remember the slow, which seems like forever process of going to the orthodontics office once a month, month after month, only to sit there while he tightened the braces ever so slightly, but certainly enough for my gums to be sore for the next few days. Month after month, which went on for years, but at the time, it felt like a lifetime? It seemed like I was never going to get these things out of my mouth. Every time I would go to the office, I would ask the doctor, "How much longer". He never really answered the question, but just sort of danced around it with some technical words that I did not understand. However, one day I did ask the doctor a technical question and surprisingly he answered with a technical answer that I understood and the Lord brought back to my remembrance. I asked the doctor why I could not just come back once a week to tighten the braces, this way the process would be speeded up and I could finally get these things off. Who cares if my mouth was going to be sore week after week to the point that I could only eat oatmeal and mashed potatoes? The answer that the doctor gave me is the same answer that God now gives me every time I begin to lose my patience in dealing with the process of changes in the way I think. The doctor told me that if he attempted to move my teeth to another position too quickly, the natural defense of my body would begin to build bone in front of the path that we want the tooth to move. My body does not want to change the position of my teeth, therefore, by moving the teeth ever so slowly; the body is unaware of the change. This is just like my mind. I say, "Change, I want change Lord", but when change comes too fast, I resist change, and begin to build a roadblock in my mind. Therefore, ever so slowly, by reading and acting on God's word daily, change is happening; even so, it may be undetectable by me, but not to others.

Therefore, laying aside all malice, all deceit, hypocrisy, envy, and all evil speaking, as newborn babes, desire the pure milk of the word, that you may grow…
1st Peter 2: 1

The other thing the Lord pointed out is to stop complaining about the process and to place my hope fully on Him, knowing that when it is completed, I can smile. The day I got those braces off, I was smiling with a smile that was like a fire that blazed the room. It was tough, it was slow, it was painful at times, but it was worth it! I would do it again if I had to! God wants us to change, change from the filthy, sin filled, selfish people that we are, to the image of His Son. However, change takes time.

And do not be conformed to the world, but be transformed by the renewing of your mind, that you may prove what is good and acceptable and the perfect will of God.
Romans 12: 2

...Just as Christ loved the church and gave Himself for her, that He might sanctify and cleanse her with the washing of water by the word of God.

I will put My law in their minds and write it on their hearts, and I will be their God, and they will be My people.
Jeremiah 31: 33

By the power of His word, God transforms us from dead dust, to a living spirit. God does the work; all we have to do is apply His word in our lives. It may take some time, dedication, work and at times some discomfort, but we can rest assured, God knows what He is doing. Trust Him!

I will instruct you and teach you in that way which you should go; I will guide you with My eye. Be not as the horse, or the mule, which has no understanding; whose mouth must be held in with a bit and bridle...
Psalms 32: 8, 9

The Important Part

Then Paul dwelt two whole years in his own rented house, and received all who came to him, preaching the Kingdom of God and teaching the things which concern the Lord Jesus Christ with all confidence, no one forbidding him.
Acts 28: 30 & 31

I believe in this Scripture God reveals to us the most important and the most rewarding gift in life, and that is sharing the good news of Jesus Christ. Here we see a man named Paul, who God had given some of the most in depth understanding of His nature. Paul had been saved by a manifestation of God. He had seen visions of heaven. God used him to heal the sick and raise the dead. Paul had witnessed to some of the most prominent people in the ruling government. He was used by God to establish churches and to help make them grow, and wrote most of the New Testament Scriptures. Yet, the book of Acts leaves Paul in a rented house preaching the Gospel to anyone that came to him.

I think that Paul had so much to offer the church. He would have made a great pastor, but God revealed to Paul the most important part. It is not a position in leadership, not a title where as others might say, 'You see him, he is very important.' Paul was interested in one thing, and that was sharing Jesus Christ his Savior with others. It did not seem to matter to Paul whether it was in his rented house, on a street corner or in a temple, Paul wanted to share what God had revealed to him. When Paul was locked up in jail he would say, "I'm free." When they threatened to kill him, he would say, ' I'm already dead.' When they tried to accuse him, he would defend the Lord Jesus. I believe that Paul came to a true revelation, that no matter where he was, what he had to do or what evil came against him, he was in peace as long as he had Jesus. It did not matter that at times all hell was breaking out around him, because he was living in the peace of God. So what is the secret? How can any person live in such a peace? Paul was truly a person who understood eternity. When we lose sight of eternity, the present seems so important to us. The world races after positions, titles, and fame because they have no hope for eternity.

Nevertheless, if we truly believe that one day we will leave here (not to a non-existence state), but to live forever in the very presence of God, the present does not seem very important. The world chases after the present because it is all that they have. They have no faith, no hope, no eternal understanding. However, a person who has been touched by God now knows in their hearts that one day their spirits will soar into His arms. I believe that Jesus welcomes every believer with tears of joy into the kingdom of Heaven. For it was this reason Jesus Christ died and was raised from the dead. I know our ego's tell us that we need to be someone in a high position, but it's funny how this man Paul, after all he went through, was not placed in a high position by God, but was sent to continue to preach and teach the Gospel of Jesus Christ. Paul came to the realization that nothing compares to God. It was not some high position, not some large earnings, or not a name of fame to show how important he was. Paul's mission was to witness for Christ.

Are we so tied up in our circumstances that we lose sight of God? Do we start to worry about our positions, our status, or our bank accounts and retirement funds and lose sight of eternity? Everything in this world will pass quickly; including our bodies, but the promise of God, His word lives forever. In that promise is the assurance that we can live in the peace of God, knowing that we are only passing through, on our way home to eternity with our loving God and Savior. That is the most important part, that one day we will be home, by the avenue of faith, as we run with endurance.

For when your faith is tested, your endurance has a chance to grow. So let it grow, for when your endurance is fully developed, you will be strong in character and ready for anything.
James 1: 3 & 4

Worship or Noise?

Take away from me the noise of your songs, for I will not hear the melody of your stringed instruments. But let justice run down like water, and righteousness like a mighty stream.
Amos 5:23 & 24

God revealed to Amos that although groups of people, even chosen people come together to worship God, their worship and praise could be in vain. In the above Scripture, the prophet heard the word of the Lord about a nation who was drifting farther and farther away from the Creator. The people were still gathering every Sabbath, but not in faith. We know this because of what God's response is to the assembly. God called their songs nothing but noise. God goes on to tell Amos that He will not listen. God makes a very strong point in saying that worship is not just on Sunday morning. The Lord goes on to say through Amos that if the people live in His justice and righteousness, the worship and praise will surely be accepted. But if we praise God on Sunday, have no faith Monday through Saturday, then all we are doing is making noise on Sunday! We cannot live in the justice and righteousness of God, who is Jesus Christ, without faith. Faith is what says I believe God! I believe Him over the newspapers, I believe Him over the special news reports, and I believe Him over opinions or viewpoints that do not agree with God's word. God is looking for believers with faith. Moreover, faith in God will change our thoughts and actions, even Monday through Saturday. Yes, we can shout and scream and clap our hands and stomp our feet in church. However, God makes it very clear that a person who truly believes and worships Him will walk in the justice and the righteousness of His ways, and not just on Sunday, but everyday. In addition, if we do not trust in God's word and follow His instructions, God tells us that our singing, our shouting, and all the sounds from the instruments are in vain. God calls it noise, an annoying sound. God seeks people who are willing to worship Him with their lives, and to achieve this, there must be a true submission to His will. This is in no way a defeat, since God is not our enemy. This is called love. Surrender in submission is certainly an act of love. Now it is easy to accept Jesus as our Savior. After all, He went through the suffering and pain of the cross. It is easy to say and believe what Jesus did as they slammed the nails in His body. After all, Jesus did it. But are we willing to believe God with our bodies? Are we willing to stop doing something we know is sin? God says we can, if we are willing to let God's righteousness govern our lives. The day that Jesus Christ died on the cross, He paid for all our sins, and once a debt is paid, there are no longer payments to be made; you are free from debt. God says; use this freedom for justice and righteousness, and this will glorify God!

*But now that you have been **set free from sin** having become slaves to God, the benefit you will reap **leads to holiness**, and the result is eternal life. Romans 6:22*

The fact that we have been forgiven for our sins, set free from the chains of shame and given a faithful promise by God of eternal life, which leads us to His holiness, is reason enough to live in thankfulness toward God. What better gift could God have given us? The appreciation we have toward God will bring us into the justice of His waters, and the streams of His righteousness. Because the gift of eternal life and the forgiveness of sins has been paid in full by the blood of Jesus Christ. What greater gift could there be? Our worship and praise to the one and only God, who has given us life when we were dead, set us free when we were imprisoned, deserves all the glory forever! If we can keep our eyes on the awesome gift that God has already given us, our spirits will rise every day in thankfulness to God who spared no expense to pay the price for our sin. Worship God with thankfulness and this will certainly bring peace and joy to our hearts, knowing that our eternal future is secure. Praise God for how He has already demonstrated His love for us in saving us from an eternal judgment. That is something we should sing, dance, and shout about with the joy of knowing that our eternal future is sealed in His nail scarred hands. That is something that we should realize every day, with every heartbeat and every breath. God's love is deep and full of His everlasting mercy. God's love is worthy of all our praise and worship.

Therefore, my heart is glad, and my glory rejoices; my flesh also will rest in hope. You will show me the path of life; in your presence is fullness of joy.   Psalm 16:9 & 11

It is not from the music or the song, but from the heart that we can worship God daily, even in all of our circumstances. Why can the redeemed spirit sing to the Lord even in times of despair? How can the saved soul still have a song for the Lord in their hearts even in times of persecution and hardship? The redeemed spirit, the saved soul knows that these temporary pains of sorrow are for but a brief moment in time compared to the endless span of eternity. This is not to minimize the hurts of this life, or to ignore that they exist. The sufferings of this life are real and can take us to a place of grieving darkness. But even in that state, there is the light of hope in Christ that is able to shine into our spirits and stabilize our souls. Yes, it still hurts, but the hope of God reminds us that all in this life is temporary, but He waits in eternity for us, where sorrow will find no place to dwell.

Offer the sacrifices of righteousness, and put your trust in the Lord.

They shall call the peoples to the mountain; there, they shall offer the sacrifices of righteousness; for they shall partake of the abundance of the seas and the treasures hidden in the sand.

But seek first the kingdom of God and His righteousness, and all these things shall be added on to you.

With the sacrifice of righteousness, we can offer the sacrifice of praise. Therefore, I will offer sacrifices of joyous shouts in His tabernacle; I will sing, yes, I will sing praises to the Lord.

Psalm 4: 5, Deuteronomy 33: 19, Matthew 6: 33,

Psalm 27: 6

Bless the Lord

Bless the Lord, O my soul: and all that is within me. Bless His holy name! Bless the Lord, O my soul and forget not all His benefits.

Psalm 103: 1, 2
This Psalm of David lifts the Lord with honor and praise. All that was in David, every cell was saying; thank you Lord for your mercy! Moreover, the Holy Spirit is quick to remind David and us that there are benefits that belong to the believer, the one who trust and worships God.

Who forgives all you iniquities, who heals all your diseases, who redeems your life from destruction, who crowns you with loving kindness and tender mercies?   Psalm 103: 3 & 4
This is how God defines the benefits of everyone that belongs to Him, who trust in His name. He offers the forgiveness of sins, for only God and God alone can forgive sins, and here we read that God does! God is also the one and only healer, since He is the Creator of these earthly bodies, it is no great task for Him to heal the very bodies that He created. God is our only Savior. Who else can save us from eternal destruction? No one but God can save us! Not only does He save us from destruction, but then He crowns those who trust Him with His love, His mercies, and His kindness.

Who satisfies your mouth with good things, so that your youth is renewed like the eagles?
Psalm 103: 5
All good things come from God. In His *loving kindness* toward us, He gives us those things that we do not deserve; He delights in giving us good things. God will put food in our mouth to strengthen our bodies and His word in our hearts that will renew our minds.

The Lord executes righteousness and justice for all who are oppressed.
Psalm 103: 6
The Lord will also see that justice is executed. How many times do we see many people who reject God, yet they seem to have the things this world offers? How many times do we see that

person constantly acting against the word of the Lord, yet they still have their health, money, and high positions? God assures us that justice belongs to Him. He is the final judge. So, pray for those who appear to be blessed, but are awaiting the final judgment.

He made known His ways to Moses, His acts to the children of Israel. The Lord is gracious, slow to anger, and abounding in mercy. Psalm 103: 7 & 8

It was only through the promise of Abraham that the nation of Israel would be born. However, the promise of His salvation by the Lord's mercy, His giving nature is now *abounding* to accept that entire are willing to receive Him. I like the word *abounding* that is used here. It means is to have plenty, more than enough, over flowing, God is *abounding in mercy* toward every person who believes in Him. His divine love for us is plentiful, without end, forever flowing. God reveals His nature to us in this Scripture. Yes, He loves, yes, He is *merciful,* yes, He is *gracious,* and *slow to anger.* It does not say that God never gets angry. It says that He is *slow to anger.* This tells us that God could get angry at the sins of a person, a family or even a nation. However, even if He does become angry with His children, His anger passes if we repent and His love for us remains forever.

He will not always strive with us, nor will He keep His anger forever. He has not dealt with us according to our sins, nor punished us according to our iniquities. Psalm 9 & 10

Can any one of us say that we deserve God's mercy? Can any one of us say that we are getting what we really deserve?

For as the heavens are high above the earth, so great is His mercy toward those who fear Him; as far as the East is from the West, so far He removed our transgressions from us. Psalm 103: 11

God reminds us when He forgives our sins in true repentance; our sins are totally forgotten. God says that He does remove our sins from us. To forgive is to forget. If we say that we forgive someone yet we refuse to forget what happened, then we really did not forgive. God defines forgiveness as forgotten, removed, washed away. He remembers them no more!

As a father pities his children, so the Lord pities those who fear Him. For He knows our frame; He remembers that we are dust. *Psalm 103: 13 & 14*
The Almighty God, our Heavenly Father who created us from the dust of the earth, knows what we are made from. He knows and understands our frame, our makeup. God knows our weaknesses and our shortcomings, He knows all about us. *As for man, his days are like grass; as a flower of the field, so he flourishes. For the wind passes over it, and it is gone, and its place remembers it no more. Psalm 103: 15 &16*
God gives us a snapshot of this life. We are here today, but we do not know whether we will be here in the next hour. Even if we all lived to be one hundred years old, it is as a short season compared to eternity. David knew this all too well. That is why David hears the Holy Spirit ministering to him to; *"Praise the Lord."* Each one of our lives is in His hands, Year to year, day-by-day, hour to hour, second by second. God calls us while we are in these bodies and then when we are released from them, He will take us home. God rules and governs all of heaven and earth, the entire universe and our life spans.
David knew he was in safe hands. On and on we could go listing the names throughout the beginning of humanity who knew that God is the only Redeemer.
Praise the Lord for He is full with compassion and mercy. His undying, unfailing and faithful love for us goes beyond all barriers of time. His desire to share His love with us knows no end, it is endless, and neither can it be limited. God's hand is extended toward us every day. He invites us into His presence; where we can find the joy, peace and assurance to say with all our hearts and minds, *bless the Lord!*

Greater Love

Greater Love has no one than this, that he lay down his life for his friends.
John 15:13

A friend told me a true story about one of his uncles who is very well educated, very intelligent and lived in a distant land. This man taught as a college professor for a very well known university. He was greatly compensated in many ways for his knowledge. He was very well paid, had the summer months off and the university would even pay for his vacations. He had everything he could ask for; money, family, a prominent position, and he was highly respected by all that knew him. He also had a lovely daughter, a daughter whom he loves very much. As it turns out in the land where he lived, only males were allowed to attend college. Females could only have an education up to the completion of high school. The daughter wanted so much to go to college; she wanted to learn so much more. So, instead of just sending the daughter to another country by herself to attend college, because of his great love for his daughter, he decided to leave his job, his country, and his home to relocate to another country where his daughter could receive a higher education. He was willing to give up all that he had to fulfill his daughter's dream. The man moved to another country with his wife and daughter. His new life was much harder than it was before. A new country, new language, new customs, everything was new. He could not find a job for over a year, and of course, even when he did find one it was nothing like the job he had back home. Again, he was willing to sacrifice for his daughter's dream. Well the daughter goes to college and when she is there, she meets a boy who had a rebellious spirit and convinces the daughter to rebel against her parents and run away with him. How do your think that father felt? Did not the daughter realize how much her father had sacrificed for her? Did she not think what this would do to her father? Most of us would ask, how could she do such a terrible thing?

Let me return to the Scripture in the beginning of this story. The word of God tells us that Jesus was with the Father in

Heaven before He came to this world. Yet, He was willing to leave His position, leave His throne to become a man here on earth. Jesus was willing to sacrifice His position in God because He loved us as the Father loves us. Just like the father who was willing to give up all that he had for his daughter, so Jesus left His heavenly throne for us.

Once here on earth, again Jesus was willing to take on the punishment for the sins of the world, so we would escape the due payment for the sins we committed. Jesus becomes a living sacrifice, a payment for man's rebellion against God. Out of love, He was willing to die a painful death. He was willing to again leave all behind so we could have eternal life.

But because of His great love for us, God, who is rich in mercy, made us alive with Christ even when we were dead in transgressions, it is by grace you have been saved.
Ephesians 2:4

Just as that father had made a decision to give his daughter all he could, so God gave all, so we might live forever. And just as the daughter decided to listen to a rebellious spirited boy, so all of mankind believed the lie of a rebellious angel and rebelled against a loving Creator who sacrificed His Son so we might live. How sad to think that the daughter did not even consider all her father did for her. How much sadder it is to think that although many people know what God has done for them, they rebel against Him, into the arms of a rebellious spirit, who wants nothing less than to kill the very people Christ died for. It is a pity to take for granted what God has done for us.

For Christ died for sins once for all, the righteous for the unrighteous, to bring you to God.
And being found in the appearance of a man, He (Christ) humbled Himself and became obedient to the point of death, even death on a cross.
Peter 3:18, Philippians 2: 8

Out of the Boat

"Lord save me!"
Matthew 14: 30
This shortest prayer ever recorded in the Scriptures is one that most of us have prayed at one time in our lives. This prayer is spoken with desperation, a cry for help when we are out of options, out of solutions and out of strength. If someone would tell me that they have never needed to use this prayer, I would tell them to just wait, because it is not over here until our bodies are in the grave, your turn will come.

The text of the above verse comes from a drowning man, going down in the deep waters of uncertainty, fearful that the raging sea of the unknown was about to swallow him up. Matthew and Mark both record this event as God reveals to us that at any given time, circumstances in our lives may quickly change from what is the normal, to a roller coaster ride of a disaster.

The chapter tells us that as the disciples were in a boat sailing to the other side of the sea; they saw Jesus walking on the water. We all know that this defies logic, the laws of gravity, and is against human ability. Nevertheless, Jesus did it, since the laws of nature do not bind him. While all the other disciples were crying like infants at this supernatural sight, most likely behind Peter, Peter steps up to the plate and says, *"Lord, if it is you, command me to come to you on the water."* Peter had guts, faith and was willing to risk what little safety he had in the boat to know if what he saw was indeed Jesus walking on water. Jesus says, *"Come,"* and Peter begins to walk on the water. However, once out of the boat, Peter looks around at the water under his feet, and the wind around him, fear sets in like frostbite, and Peter begins to sink like a weight. As Peter is disappearing in the black sea, he prays the only prayer that he knew, *"Lord, help me!"*

What is interesting about this event is that none of the other disciples that were safe in the boat prayed any prayer at all, because there was no threat of drowning. It seems that with most of us, as long as we are safe in our daily routines, in the boat where the troubled waters cannot touch us, there is no need to give God much thought. However, when we find our little worlds in a tailspin of heartbreak, we quickly remember God. Unfortunately, I would go so far as to say that the crises in our lives are the very times that draw us closer to God. It is somewhat sad to think that we make ourselves our own god while in the safety of our little boats. We make all our decisions based on our opinions, and the opinions of others, and ignore God until we are in deep trouble, instead of basing our decisions on God's instructions first. And when we fail, we are quick to blame God. God is not the cause of our troubles. We do have an enemy, Satan. However, he has no power over us, except for the authority we give him, as Adam and Eve so carelessly traded for a bite of the forbidden fruit.

We will all experience out of the boat traumas that will turn our worlds upside down, some of us might even experience more than a few. However, as we see from the experience of Peter, Jesus Christ is willing and very able to extent His hand of mercy in any drowning state that we might find ourselves sinking in the sea of doubt. For we will all discover that in these times of trouble, our own strength will only take us so far, before the seams in our minds begin to come apart, and then we find ourselves more in a panic than when we first started. Above all the other thoughts of fear that might cloud our reasoning in these times of pain, sorrow and confusion, we can hold on to the rock of God's love for us, through His Son, Jesus Christ. For it was Jesus who Peter called out to for help as he found himself in a situation that was about to pull him under. Jesus is the same today, as yesterday, and forever. He knows our struggles, and He certainly knows our hearts. He also suffered, and He knows the pains of our tragedies. Jesus tells us to believe in Him, and call upon His name, for His ear is open to the prayer in faith.

"Let not your hearts be troubled; you believe in God, believe in Me also."

"...Jesus is waiting for your call, because He loves you right now, even into eternity!

Always Confident

Therefore we are always confident and know that as long as we are at home in the body we are away from the Lord. We live by faith, not by sight. We are confident; I say and would prefer to be away from the body and at home with the Lord. So we make it our goal to please Him, whether we are at home in the body or away from it.
2nd Corinthians 5:6-9

God reveals to us through the Apostle Paul that we should live in the confidence of faith, knowing that faith pleases God. However, concerning the death of our bodies, we still seem to hold on to the fear of death, which is a faith failure. God tells us to be confident and know, no guessing, no wondering, but knowing without a doubt what is in store for us when these mortal bodies give out.

What does the word death mean and how does it apply to those who believe, not according to opinions, but by the word of the living God? God tells us about a first death and a second death. Without understanding the word of God, we will never realize the events that will take place when our bodies die. By God's word, we can live free from the fear of death and live by the confidence of faith, knowing where we will be at that moment in time when God calls us out of the natural and into the spiritual realm. Death in both the first and the second definitions are separation. The first death is the separation of the spirit from the body. The second death is separation from God. God does not tell us that death is a non-existent state! When our bodies die, our spirits are separated from our bodies and we are then at *home with the Lord.* There should be no wavering of doubt in that fact. God tells us that we should have the most confidence in this hope. There should be no second-guessing about what happens to a believer when the separation of the body and spirit takes place!

Now let us look at God's word to prove that what God said to the apostle is true. The first of many examples on the separation of our spirits and bodies, and where our spirits will go at the time of our departure is given to us when Jesus was on the cross. There were two criminals hung with him, one on each side. The one man says these wonderful words to our Lord:

"Jesus remember me when you come into your kingdom."
Luke 23:42

This man, though drowning is his own sins, showed Jesus a spark of faith, calling out our Lord's name and acknowledging that He is a King and He will enter into His kingdom. This man showed no doubt, no unbelief; the word is confidence. He was confident about where Jesus was going. This man had no training, no ministry, and no church to support him. He had no pastor who he could run to for advice. He did not have the word of God printed in a book so he could reference any subject. Nevertheless, he did have faith; given from God in the knowledge that Jesus is who He says He is. With that spark of faith, Jesus gives him and us an answer that should give us the confidence in faith of what happens when we as believers are separated from these bodies.

Jesus answered him, "I tell you the truth, today, you will be with Me in paradise."
Luke 23:43

What wonderful words, and what an awesome promise from the mouth of God. We can have confidence that when the day comes for our spirits to separate from our bodies, we will be in paradise with Jesus, in the awesome presence of God. Is there any other promise that we can think of that should melt away the fear of the death of these bodies? Like a snake that sheds its skin, so we shall shed these fleshly bodies, and the eternal in our spirits will then be seen and understood. The awesome, powerful promise of Jesus Christ should echo in our minds, in that we have a ticket to paradise, an express shuttle that will deliver us to a place that the bible tells us we could not even be able to describe in the present form of communication. No matter what, the ticket once accepted cannot be taken away, but can certainly be walked away from, by free choice.

As it was revealed to the Apostle Paul and the criminal on the cross beside Jesus, the ticket into the kingdom of God can only be received by faith. The man, whose name is not mentioned, did not live a holy life, and did not follow the Law of Moses as to purchase the ticket of eternal life through deeds. He was not a member of a ministry or even any organized religion as far as we know. This man received the free gift, the ticket to life through a confession of faith, even right before the separation of his body and spirit was about to take place. This is by no means condoning us to live any way we want, and then confess Christ at the very end of our lives. This confidence from faith should cause us to walk in acts of faith, not shaken, not failing, but doubtless in the knowledge of what God has in store for those who believe. God tells us plainly:

It is better to trust in the Lord than to put confidence in man.
Psalm 118:8

Is our confidence in God or man? God tells us to place our confidence, apply our faith in Him alone.

We can settle the issue in our minds that the second death has no power over the believer, because Jesus paid the price for all our sins on the cross. As for the criminal, although his legs were broken, and his was body dead and buried, his spirit is in paradise with Jesus at this very moment. The Apostles Paul, Peter, James and so many believers were more than willing to lay down their lives for the One who gave His life for all. They all had confidence in the hope of the promise of eternal life in the presence of God. If this were not true then the sacrifice of Jesus on the cross would have been in vain! Therefore, we can build a house of confidence, anchored on the Rock of our Savior, firmly footed on the promise of God.

In the Gospel of John, Jesus gives us the most reassuring promise that should release the fear of death and ensure our minds with confidence.

Do not let your hearts be troubled. Trust in God; trust also in Me. In My Father's house are many rooms; if it were not so, I would have told you. I am going there to prepare a place for you.
John 14:1

What another awesome promise given to us by our Lord Jesus Christ! Jesus is telling us as plainly as it can be said, do not be *troubled,* and tormented with the fear of the separation of the body and spirit. Trust God with confidence that Jesus Himself has prepared a place for us for an eternal life with Him. No matter how many trials we might go through while we are here, they are nothing compared to what Jesus has prepared for those who trust in Him. Know the truth, and the truth will set you free. And the truth is that those who trust in Jesus Christ will by no means be disappointed. Jesus adds something that is very important and that should be kept in the heart of every believer!

I will not leave you as orphans; I will come to you. Because I live, you also will live.
John 4: 18 & 19

God is faithful and can be trusted. He will make every promise a reality, for God is pure and holy, He cannot lie.
For the Lord will not cast off His people, nor, will He forsake His inheritance.
Psalm 94:14
Those who are planted in the house of the Lord shall flourish in the courts of our God
Psalm 92: 13
The Lord has made known His salvation...
All the ends of the earth have seen the salvation of God.
Psalm 98: 2, 3

Trusting is a giving of self, surrender in love that leaves behind the fears in doubts, in a bonding to another without a second thought of betrayal. It is holding nothing back, but submitting into that trust, knowing that the person we trust is faithful and has our best interest in heart. God's salvation in Jesus Christ is the ultimate proof that God can be trusted, not only in the problems of this life, but for eternity.
All the paths of the Lord are mercy and truth.
Psalms 25: 10

The Days of Man

As for man, his days are like grass; as a flower of the field, so he flourishes. For the wind passes over it, it is gone, and its place remembers it no more.
  Psalm 103:15 & 16

Our days are but a short season. Like the seed that is conceived in the fall, nurtured in the winter, and comes to a new life in the spring. The seed breaks through the ground. It now feels the ray of the sun, and it drinks the falling mist of water. It now knows it is alive, and all of creation takes notice. Bright, sun filled days with cool rain brings the life out through the soil. Before long it is standing tall and strong, unshaken by the winds. Into the summer it goes. Days filled with warm breezes and nights of renewing showers. Day after day, and night after night the flower stands in glory, a clear reflection of what is in the heart of the Creator.

Then the days become shorter, not as warm and the showers are now turning much colder. The stems that stood so strong and tall begin to stoop and bend. The morning dew is replaced by frost, and now the flower, weak and worn begins to draw closer to the earth where it came from. For the season is over, its time is now past. Into the ground it falls when the final wind passes over it. It is seen no more, it is forgotten and replaced by another.

For what is your life? It is even a vapor that appears for a little time and then vanishes away,
James 4: 14

As the season of a flower, so man's life passes by, says the Lord. Nevertheless, unlike the flower, the Creator has a special place in His heart for humanity. We finish our course and pass through our season, but unlike the flower, we have been given a spirit that knows the Maker. This spirit yearns to be joined with the One who is the *Father of all spirits.* Then the spirit, no longer imprisoned by the body, it is set free. It begins to travel through the barriers of time to God, who welcomes the spirit with open arms of love, stored up from the beginning of creation. Joy is heard throughout all of heaven, a child of the Most High has come home. The Creator rejoices with nail-scarred hands and feet, He breaks out with laughter. Never to be separated again, the Creator and the creation, forever together.

Having been born again, not of a corruptible seed but incorruptible, through the word of God which lives and abides forever.

1st Peter 1: 23

As creation was brought forth through a word, so our eternal, incorruptible seed is brought forth through the same word, the word of God. God's word is eternal *and the word became flesh.* Jesus is the eternal word of God. Therefore, faith in Him brings forth eternal life in the inner man (the spirit), but the flesh, which is corruptible, will die.

Certainly every man at his best is but a vapor.

Surely every man is a vapor.

Psalm 39: 5, 11

As the flower is a man's life, it is here for only a season. The Scripture says that at *his best*, at the very best he could be, he is only a vapor, a mist that is here for but a moment. However, unlike the flower, the season ends, but eternity begins. For an eternal seed is planted and nurtured in the dust of flesh, waiting to break forth to feel the warmth of God's love. It is sown in corruptible ground, the flesh, but is raised in an incorruptible glory in the spirit. Much like the caterpillar, who crawls into the cocoon, begins a complete transformation, and then flies out as a butterfly, no longer crawling, but flying! No longer bound to the earth, but now free in the heavens. This is simply the truth for all those that place their trust in Christ.

For you died, and your life is hidden with Christ in God. When Christ, who is your life, appears, then you will also appear with Him in glory.

Colossians 3:3 & 4

Therefore, if any man be in Christ, he is a new (born again), *creature: old things are passed away; behold, all things are become new.*

2nd Corinthians 5:17

Born to Him

Moreover, you took your sons and daughters, whom you bore to Me, and these you sacrificed to them to be devoured.
...That you have slain My children and offered them up by causing them to pass through the fire.
...You did not remember the days of your youth, when you were naked and bare, struggling in your blood.
...Says the Lord God.
Ezekiel 16: 20 – 23

The prophet Ezekiel receives a word from the heart of God concerning the murdering of babies. The word murder, destroy, devoured, can be phrased together to mean all the same thing, to stop life. God makes a very clear statement in telling us that children should not be destroyed and thrown away as a paper towel. God tells us that we bore our children unto Him and God decided to give the child life and that child is His. Children are not born out of the will of a man or women, but out of the will of God. Out of the thousands and thousands of sperm cells, one sperm races to find the waiting egg, hidden deep in the body. God guides that one sperm, the one He has chosen to live, and that one sperm produced you or I. A child is not chosen from a man and a woman, because they have decided to make love with each other, but because God decided to conceive a new life. We are all here because of the will of God. There are no accidents, no mistakes, no one who was not planned by God. If anyone has been conceived, it is from the will of God. Once that sperm becomes united with the egg, the struggle to live begins. God tells us that we do not remember, but He does and reminds us that it is a struggle.

In that one cell, there is more information than a room full of books. The very blueprint of our structure is all drawn out, our hands, our feet, our legs, our eyes, our ears, and our mouths, all pictured in that one cell, ready to be formed cell by cell. God is the Master Craftsman as He calls out
: "Live! Yes I said to you in your blood, live!"
Ezekiel 16:6

When God says live, life will take place. Each one of us has received the command from God to live. For without that command there would be no life.

Each one of us is one of a kind. In all the trillions and trillions of people born through the course of history, no one is like you. There was never a copy of you born before you existed and there will never be a copy of you in the future. You are one of a kind. No two people throughout humanity have been duplicated. Even identical twins are not exactly the same. God makes every one of us special, one by one. God also makes it very clear that we belong to Him. Do we have the right to stop what God has commanded to live? Do we know more than God does? What greater sin could there be? God has formed us, each one of us, and commanded us to live. Who are we to say no? Who are we to prevent the plan of God?

God also tells us that the things we do to others will certainly return to us whether they are for good or evil.

"Because you did not remember the days of your youth, but agitated me with all these things, surely I will recompense your deeds on your own head," says the Lord God.
Ezekiel 16:43

What we do comes back to us like a rubber ball we throw against a wall, it returns. Do not think for one moment that a decision to abort a child is an act that will be finished once the baby is gone. That act, the rubber ball will return. It is an act against God, because God Himself calls that baby His. Do not deny those eyes to know tears of joy, or the mouth to be denied the smiles of laughter, or those ears to hear the word of the living God. It could have happened to you or me. Maybe someone could have denied us life. Just think for one moment, how many other lives that would have affected. All life is the will of God. We have no right to say kill what God has commanded to live. There is no reasoning, no questioning, and no doubting this fact; the child's blood is on the hands of the one who murders.

The voice of your brother's blood cries out to Me from the ground.
Genesis 4:10
Rather than put blood in the ground, put faith in your heart, that God can do all things if we only believe. God commands life and He asks us to believe in life, because He is life, the Giver and Sustainer of all life, the Author of all life. Moreover, without Him, nothing lives!
For you formed my inward parts; you covered me in my mother's womb.
My frame was not hidden from you.
When I was made in secret. Your eyes saw my substance, being yet formed.
Psalm 139:13, 15, 16
Can a woman forget her sucking child, that she should have compassion on the son of her womb? Yes, they may forget, yet I will not forget you.
Isaiah 49: 15
Children are a heritage of the Lord; and the fruit of the womb is His reward.
Psalm 127: 3
How much more does God have to say concerning the value of life in the womb?
Man's opinion is foolishness, ignorant concerning the gift of life that has been granted by God in the womb of a mother. Who should deny the life that God has commanded to live?
There is a way that seems right to a man, but its end is the ways of death.
Proverbs 16:25

God Has a Plan

In the heart a man plans his course, but the Lord determines his steps.
Proverbs 16:9

We all try to plan our lives in short and long term goals. We plan for this and plan for that, thinking we are charting our own course. Nevertheless, in the above Proverb, God tells us that He alone is the one who determines each step.

Commit to the Lord whatever you do, and your plans will succeed.
Proverbs 16:3

Here we see God make a promise to all that are willing to place their trust in Him. He tells us that if we commit to Him whatever we are doing, according to His commands, it will succeed.

You might ask, how is it that even unbelievers are successful, prosperous and secure in wealth.

To answer that question we have to understand what God's definition of success is. God does not care about your position in IBM, or even your position as a church leader. If you are not giving Him the glory for it, then it does not matter to God. God does not look at success as the world sees it. The world sees success as money, position, and power. God says that to Him we are a success if we are living in His will. If we are willing to be a disciple of God, then we are a success in God's eyes. That is how God defines success! Forget about the money, position and so-called power. God says that the real riches, true position and super power come from the wealth of knowing Him. Wealth is in the position of being able to walk with Him, and living in the powerful victory of a true child of the living God. It is true that some people might have obtained money, but with it will come troubles, if you are out of God's will. Yes, some have obtained great positions as high-ranking officials. However, without knowing Christ, your position is worthless. In the natural, those who have obtained wealth seem to be so happy and seem to have so much freedom. However, in the spiritual realm, they are decayed, shipwrecked, lost and stumbling in darkness without Christ, and slaves to the darkness of sin. Their spirits are lifeless, and their hearts have grown dark and cold. They are so far removed from the living God, because they have chosen to worship the riches of this world, making pleasure and material possessions their idols. How could they really be happy? Many people can put on a smile and say things are great, but God knows the heart. If they have no faith in the Creator, then they are in chains, trapped in a spiritual dungeon of hopelessness.

Before this faith came, we were held prisoners by the law, locked up until faith should be revealed. Galatians 3:23

Not all the money, position, and power can release us from being prisoners under the burden of sin. Only faith in the living God through Jesus Christ can free us from those chains of doubt, from the cells of unbelief that decays our spirits like a cancer. Only by faith in God, by His mercy, can anyone be free from the hold of sin that separates us from God. Do not think that achievements of position, power and wealth will mean anything when we leave here and stand before the eternal Judge. He will not be interested in our titles, retirement funds, or our level of academics. We can gain all the knowledge that the world says is valuable to know. We can earn degree after degree and academic achievements to be the most prominent and respected person around. Yet, if we have not gained any knowledge of God, if we have escaped God's will and forsaken His wisdom, if we have rejected His mercy, defiled His love and disowned His grace, we have less than nothing!

God's mercy was shown by sending His Son Jesus Christ to the cross to pay a ransom for sin that we were unable to pay. Our spiritual bank accounts fell way short of the price of sin, leaving us in spiritual bankruptcy. There is no way we could have paid that debt; it was just too much for humanity. To be in God's will, and to gain the true wisdom that is a clear result of knowing Him, without the acceptance of the sacrifice Jesus made on the cross, is simply impossible. What could be a greater success than having eternal life? *Jesus declared,*

"For I have come down from heaven not to do my will but to do the will of Him who sent me."

For the Father's will is that everyone who looks to the Son and believes in Him shall have eternal life, and I will raise him up at the last day."
John 6:38 & 40
Do not be blinded by man's definition of success, God's definition of success is eternal life through faith in Jesus Christ. Moreover, without life, what do we really have? What can compare to life? Nothing! No, not the best made car, the biggest house, that biggest boat, the fastest jet, and the most secured stocks and bonds, could never equal one minute of life here, and even more in the eternal.
"All flesh is like grass, and all the glory (All the possessions, all the pleasures, and all the positions), *of man is like the flower of the grass. The grass withers, and the flower falls away, but the word of the Lord endures forever.*
1ˢᵗ Peter 1: 24
Although we are here for just a moment in time, God has eternal plans for us. For God always has the eternal in mind.
"For I know the plans I have for you," declares the Lord, "plans to prosper you and not to harm you, plans to give you hope and a future."
Jeremiah 29: 11
Our future in is the eternal, with the only eternal God.
The eternal God is your refuge, and underneath are the everlasting arms...
Deuteronomy 33: 27

Man and Woman

God saw all that He had made, and it was very good.
Genesis 1:31
After God created all things, including the first man Adam, God was pleased. He had placed this man in a garden of paradise to take care of it. Nevertheless, one thing was missing.
The Lord God said, "It is not good for man to be alone, I will make a helper suitable for Him."
Genesis 2:18
Here we can see God's intent for Adam and we can be sure it is the same intent for the man of today. Man needs a helper. For God Himself, the Creator of the man tells us, *it is not good to be alone.* And once the union of marriage, the bond of a covenant is confessed in the presence of God toward each other, the man and the women become one in God's eyes. Moreover, if God sees the man and woman as one, then why should not we see it the same way? What hurts the husband hurts his wife, and what gives joy to the husband gives joy to the wife since the two are one in marriage. Would a man try to hurt any members of his own body? So God tells us that the husband and wife are one, they should love and respect each other as they love and respect their own bodies.
To the man God commands:
Did not the Lord make you one with your wife?
Malachi 2:15
Again, God reminds man that the husband is one with his wife and that oneness in body and spirit belongs to God. As God is faithful, He commands the man to be faithful, loyal and loving to his wife. God Himself is the witness that the two are now one in the covenant of marriage. If the man is faithful, this will find favor with the Lord.
The man who finds a wife finds a treasure and receives favor from the Lord.
Proverbs 18:22
What a revealing word from the heart of God, to say that a man's wife is his treasure, more valuable than any treasure of gold or silver this world can offer, because with this treasure comes also the favor of God.

Says the Almighty Lord, "So guard yourself in the spirit, and do not break faith."
Malachi 2:16
Guard you treasure with a faithful commitment, in a bond of love and trust, united as one, knowing that God's favor will pour out blessing after blessing to the ones who obey and honor God's commands. If God honors the covenant of marriage so much, who are we to dishonor it? God is always ready to explain to us what is best for us, and He will always warn us of the dangers in this life.
Another thing you do: You flood the Lords altar with tears. You weep and wail because He no longer pays attention to your offerings or accepts them with pleasure from your hands. You ask why? It is because the Lord is the witness between you and your wife of your youth, because you have broken faith with her, though she is your partner, the wife of your marriage covenant. Has not the Lord made them one?
Malachi 2:13-15
"Therefore what God has joined together, let man not separate."
Mark 10:9
God's heart is revealed as He clearly tells us that there are some things that He hates and declares an injustice. Yes, the one and only God, who is love and justice, hates the act of unfaithfulness that breaks the bond of a covenant between a husband and wife, it is sin. And sin is a foul odor to God.
For God's promises to us are faithful and true, based on covenant as His commitment through Jesus Christ has delivered us from our sins. We also should have this same mind when we make a covenant in the promise of marriage. God has not forsaken us in His promise; neither should we forsake one another.
"For the Lord God of Israel says that He hates divorce, for it covers one's garment with violence."
Malachi 2: 16

The Enduro

...We ourselves boast of you among the churches of God for your patience and faith in all your persecutions and tribulations that you endure...
2nd Thessalonians 1: 3

There are tracks across the country that race modified cars in what is known as an Enduro race. The cars are equipment with special safety modifications to protect the driver from the violent aggression of the other drivers in the race, because in the Enduro Race there are no rules, anything goes. Other drivers can smash into any car at any given time during the race in attempting to throw the competition out of the run. In speaking to any one of the drivers, they will all give the same comments on the objective of the race, 'to endure to the end, and maybe even win.' While going through the smashing of the other opponents, they never lose sight of the finish line and the main objective, to endure to the end. The Holy Spirit told the Apostle Paul to run the *race of faith.* Moreover, at coming to the end of his earthly stay, Paul told Timothy that he had *finished the course.* The race that the Holy Spirit revealed to the apostle is not a race of speed, although time is certainly an opponent in our short stay here on earth. However, the race of faith is a run of endurance. In this letter to the church of the Thessalonians, God reminds the church (us), through the apostle that running the race of faith with our eyes focused on the finish line will assure us in completing the course. In the opening letter to the church, God reveals where our point of focus should be, as a sharpshooter that focuses on the target. God also reveals the undeniable truth of what is waiting for those who finish the race of faith and those that are not even in it because of their unbelief.

...Which is manifest evidence of the righteous judgment of God, that you may be counted worthy of the kingdom of God, for which you also suffer....
2nd Thessalonians 1:5

The suffering of the early church was real, as the true believers were hunted as criminals, even persecuted to the point of death. Unlike our timid version of the Christian faith today that

is easily shaken by social rejection, countless saints shed their blood so the message of Christ would survive the opposition toward the truth of the gospel. The true evidence of the coming judgment of God was in the testimony of these men and women that were willing to lay down their lives for the gospel. The early church felt honored to be a witness of the glorious salvation of God that was paid for in full by the blood of Christ Jesus. However, God goes on to assure those saints and all that believe, that at the end of the race there will be rest for those that ran to the finish, and trouble for those that did not run. For at the end of this race is where we will live our eternities with no chances to come back and re-run the course. ...Since it is a righteous thing with God to repay with tribulation those who trouble you, and to give you who are troubled rest with us when the Lord Jesus is revealed from heaven with His mighty angels in flaming fire taking vengeance on those who do not know God, and on those who do not obey the gospel of our Lord Jesus Christ.
2nd Thessalonians 1: 6 – 8
It has been said time and time again throughout the ages that there is coming a day. Whether it is the day of the Lord's return, or the day that we leave these earthly bodies, that will be the end of the Endro Race. It will be good for all those that believe and the beginning of troubles for those that do not. God tells the believer that there is rest in Him at the completed course of faith and judgment for those that decided to run their own race of pride, greed and selfishness. God makes a clear distinction between those who know Him and those who disobey the truth of the gospel. There is no hope for those who turn away from the mercy of God that was displayed on the cross by Jesus Christ, as a one-time offering for the sins of the world. There is no redemption in the good works of any soul unless they have been washed with the holy blood of the risen Savior. However, for those that believe there awaits a rest. It is not a rest of sleep, but a rest of peace that is given to all those who endure with patience, in trusting God till the end. As the Enduro Race drivers are willing to focus on the finish line to complete the course, so should we focus on the end of our course, or the

returning of the King of all kings and the Lord of all lords, Jesus Christ. For there is coming a day and on that day every one of us will stand before the throne of God and will give an account of our faith, or the absence of it.

These shall be punished with everlasting destruction from the presence of the Lord and from the glory of His power, when He comes, in that day, to be glorified in His saints and to be admired among all those who believe...
2nd Thessalonians 1: 9

We need to *keep the faith*, in good times and in bad, even when the opposition is trying desperately to throw us off course and derail our trust in the Creator. For Jesus promised us that He has prepared a place for us in the presence of God, and for all those that believe on His name and finish the race will have rest. It is a rest in God's love, and it is forever.

As the runner gasps for each breath, running the final laps, he or she sees nothing but the finish line. Although they might not be able to see the finish line physically, they see it in their hearts and minds, pressing forward, refusing to give in to the pains in their sides and legs. They know by then that the finish line is so near, they just need to keep running. So it is as our earthy bodies begin to decay and the aches and pains of a fallen nature is clearly revealed. However, in the spirit we can run stronger, faster, believing God without doubt that He is waiting for us at the finish line with nail scared hands.

Therefore, we do not lose heart. Even though our outward man is perishing, yet the inward man is being renewed day by day. For our light affliction, which is but for a moment, is working for us a far more exceeding and eternal weight of glory.
2nd Corinthians 4: 16, 17

He Loved Me with a Cross

"For God so loved the world that He gave His only begotten Son..."
John 3:16

The title is taken from a hymn that helps to bring into focus the magnitude of the awesome power of divine love, which is not based on merit, but unselfish giving. For the true definition of love, even on a human realm, is the giving of one's self to another. Although we limit the power of love to the boundaries of conditions, God does not.

This was the message that was preached in the ancient cities like Corinth, Colosse, Philippi, and Rome, These cities where no different from the cities of today, with the same murder, corruption and immorality that are read in the headlines everyday. It is the message of eternal hope, and eternal pardon from every act of sin against God and humanity. However, there was a cost, one that could never be paid by the sacrifices of men stained with the blemish of sin. The only sacrifice that could ever pay for the sin of humanity would have to be sinless, holy, untainted by the curse of rebellion.

If I can use this illustration to explain the gift of God, who is Jesus Christ, that was given as an eternal sacrifice by the pure reason of love.

Can we say that ten birds are worth as much as the life of a child? Are twenty robins worth more that a man or a woman? Can one hundred or maybe one thousand blue jays equal one human life? I think not! We could stack robins upon robins until they filled the entire universe, and they would never be equivalent to one human being, because we are speaking about a much higher order of life. However, if there were a human being, that somehow could become a bird, without ceasing to be a human being, we would have a bird that was worth more then every bird that ever existed.

This is the good news of the gift of God, that God, the eternal Son Himself came to us in the form of a man. He became one of us, born of the virgin Mary, but never ceased to be who He is, and was willing to take our punishment for our sin on the cross, and shed His blood for the sake of our pardon. That is love in the purest form.

By this we know love, because He laid down His life for us.
1st John 3: 16

The motivation behind this ultimate sacrifice was love and pure love is not a mathematical equation; it is not contained or restricted by the so-called logic of our reasoning. God's love is beyond our physics, our physiology, and certainly beyond any theology. This we know, that God loved us with a cross.

And being found in the appearance as a man, He humbled Himself and became obedient to the point of death, even the death of the cross.
Philippians 2: 8

For what the law could not do, love did, and provided a way into the presence of God, without shame or condemnation. This truth might hurt our frail egos, but God does not love us because of how great we are, or because of in some way we have earned His love through our own definition of faithfulness. God loves us because of who He is.

This is the same good news that was preached by the first followers of Christ, that He alone paid the debt for our every trespass on the cross, leaving no balance due. Any sacrifice that we might attempt to offer the Almighty for the redemption from sin would be mere pennies compared to the pure, holy, sinless blood of Jesus Christ. That sacrifice was so complete, that by faith in it alone, we are forgiven.

Behold what manner of love the Father has bestowed on us, that we should be called children of God.
1st John 3: 1

Christ has redeemed us from the curse of the law (sin), *having become a curse for us...*
Galatians 3: 13

Now, we, brethren, as Isaac was, are children of promise...
Galatians 4: 28

Lot

"Just as it was in the days of Noah, so also it will be in the days of the Son of Man. People were eating, drinking, marrying, and being given in marriage up to the day Noah entered the Ark. The flood came and destroyed them all. It was the same in the days of Lot. People were eating and drinking, buying and selling, planting and building. But the day Lot left Sodom, fire and sulfur rained down from heaven and destroyed them all. It will be just like this on the day the Son of Man is revealed."
Luke 17:26-30

Jesus gives us a snapshot of what was going on when the floods came in the days of Noah and the heavens rained fire on Sodom. In both instances, God tells us that the people were enjoying prosperity in a time of plenty. God tells us that in both times the people were eating and drinking, enjoying their harvest with no concern about their spiritual condition. They were gathering in wedding celebrations and the wine was flowing. They were buying and selling, planting and building. It sounds like they were in a great economic condition. There is no mention of food shortages. They were building for the future, investing and celebrating their success. But they were all spiritually dead. They could not hear God because they were consumed by their lust, their greed, and their selfishness. They had no idea what was happening to them. In both times, the people of those days had drifted so far away from God that they could only hear the voice of their own greed and lust. Does this picture look familiar? Of course, some people might argue that things were different back then. Well some things were different, but their sin was the same as the sin of today. Therefore, in the middle of this false security of economic success it suddenly starts to rain. In the first instance, it rains water, then the next instance it rains fire, There is no doubt that the people were caught off guard both times. Jesus reminds us that because of their sin they were caught up in a false sense of economic security and plainly ignored God. Here Jesus tells us that in the days of His return, the people of the nations will be caught up in the same false sense of economics and will ignore the one and only living God. In other words, people's lives will be going on normally. Man will think he has everything under control, although he will admit the world has some problems. But man's thinking is if we can throw enough money at the problem, we will solve it. This could be one of the biggest lies in the heart of man. If prosperity were the answer today then it would have been the answer in the days of Noah and Lot. It was not the answer then and it is not the answer now. Only God and God alone can turn the polluted heart of man around. Only God can show the people how we can grow into spiritual maturity and rest in the knowledge of His mercy, understanding how much God loves us and cares for us. As in the days of Noah and Lot, the prosperity blinded the people into believing that their lives were just fine without God's help. However, they were spiritually disconnected from their Creator, which led them into deep perversion and lust. Therefore, as the political leaders boast on how good the economic picture is for the years ahead, and they do seem to convince many about the programs that are under way, remember the words of God. *"It will be just like this on the day the Son of Man is revealed." Luke 17:30*

Real Love

*Know therefore that the Lord your God is God; He is the faithful
God, keeping His covenant of love...*
Deuteronomy 7: 9

The true definition of a real love between a man and a woman
is not based on the few moments of passion, or physical
gratification in which the world markets and sells as love. Real
love between a man and a woman is defined in the Scriptures
as *two that become one,* spiritually, mentally and yes, even
legally. God's definition of true love is based on faithfulness,
which is birth through a commitment, a *covenant of love.* I know
this might sound like foolishness in an age where freedom of
choice dominates even some of our own constitutional laws.
However, God's laws are set in place for a much better reason
then man's, and without a *covenant of love* (marriage),
between a man and a women, we violate God's command.
*Do not be deceived: neither fornicators, nor idolaters, nor
adulterers, nor homosexuals, nor sodomites, nor thieves, nor
covetous, nor drunkards, nor revilers, nor extortionists will
inherit the kingdom of God.*
1ˢᵗ Corinthians 6: 9-10

Why would God give us such a warning, placing the act of
fornication and adultery in the same category as stealing and
extortion? God knows our frail makeup, He knows that we are
vulnerable to sin, but God also knows what is best for us. For in
a country where God is expelled from public schools, barred
from courtrooms, and ignored in legislation, this society has
become their own god, judging for themselves between right
and wrong, which is like giving a five-year-old child the freedom
to choose his or her own life style. The child would be dead
before the age of twenty just by malnutrition alone.
God knows that without a covenant of marriage, there is no
faithfulness, no true unity, and no commitment, which then
leaves the dependency on physical needs, which could easily
be fulfilled by anyone. That line of thinking can hurt people, and
leave some drowning in bitterness and distrust. Without the
commitment of a promise, which is an open confession of faith
before God and to each other, we are nothing more than dogs

that are easily swayed by a quick meal. This might come to as shock to some people, but God knows much more than we will ever know. God knows everything, most of all, what is best for us, as good parents know what is best for their child. And though man might continue in rebellion against the oracles of God, he will find himself walking in the dark with emotional and spiritual bruises from his own miscalculations.

Marriage is honorable in all, and the bed undefiled: but whoremongers and adulterers God will judge.

Hebrews 13: 4

God tells us that *marriage is honorable*, maybe not before a society that wants to make up its own rules according to its own judgments, but is honorable before God, who is and will always be the Judge of all judges. God gives us commandments because He knows what is best for us and loves us, and wants the best for us. However, He cannot ignore a rebellion against His commandments, which is sin, and will judge it no matter how we might try to justify it in our own minds.

I was on an interstate when I saw a billboard that stated, "God said… God said… God said… God said… God said…God said…God said…God said… what part of that don't you understand?" I know all the atheist out there will argue concerning the authenticity of God's word. However, God has given us an owner's manual, which clearly states that the physical relations outside the boundaries of marriage is not freedom of choice, it is not freedom of self expression, and is certainly not a lasting union, but it is sin, which is in the same league as homosexuality, stealing and covertness. Therefore, the Scriptures tell us that God will judge it, like any other sin, unless we confess the sin to God, and change, therefore honoring God, and He will forgive and honor all who are willing to place Him as God in every area of their lives.

For this reason a man shall leave his father and mother and be joined to his wife, and the two will become one flesh.

Genesis 2: 24

Our Father

Have we not all one Father? Has not one God created us?
Malachi 2:10

It is interesting how God receives the title as Father. The prophet Malachi asked a question that deals with the subject. If God wants to be referred to as our Father, then we should recognize the high honor in the position of fatherhood. God views the responsibility as most important and does not take the title lightly.

God refers to Himself as Father for two reasons:

The first reason is that while we give honor to our earthly fathers (and mothers) for all their love and even our natural existence, God is no doubt the Father of our spirits and has allowed us to born in the natural and re-born in the supernatural.

The second reason is that the word father signifies a relationship. The bond between the Creator and His creation called man is as a good father that loves his child. God's intention is to reveal His love to every man, woman and child, through His personal relationship with us.

Therefore, fatherhood is not just a biological, gene connection limited by moral or legal responsibilities, but rather it is the position of a man's heart that reflects the love of God.

Jesus always referred to God the Father as Father. At the beginning of every prayer, Jesus addresses the Almighty as Father. This is not saying that Jesus is a created being. On the contrary, *all things were made through Him and for Him, and without Him nothing was made.* Jesus was not created since He was part of the Creator at the time all things were made. Does it say anywhere in the Scriptures that Jesus was created by the Father?

"For God, (the Father) *so loved the world that He gave His only begotten Son,* (Jesus)*, that whoever,* (you and I) *believes in Him,*(Jesus) *should not perish but have everlasting life."*
John 3:16

The words *only begotten,* which is one Greek word, *monogenes,* is used five times in the gospel of the Apostle John. Every time the apostle uses this word, he is referring to the relationship between the Father and the Son within the Godhead. *Monogenes* cannot be defined as born first; rather, it is a word that expresses the meaning of a relationship. In the case of the Father and the Son, the relationship is eternal with no beginning and with no end. John and the others had witnessed this relationship with their own eyes as they saw the divine nature of God heal the sick, open the eyes of the blind, restore the legs of the crippled and raise the dead. Jesus did something that only God could do; forgive the sins of the heart, which is the only thing that can give peace in the mind and real joy in the spirit.

I will be a Father to you, and you shall be My sons and daughters, says the Lord Almighty. 2^(nd) *Samuel* 7:14

This promise was given to the people of Israel that they would be God's own people and God would be their Father. The Holy Spirit brings this awesome promise into the New Covenant stating that this promise belongs to all those who believe that *God* the Father *was in Christ reconciling the world to Himself.* This does not strip Jesus Christ of His identity as the Son of God. However, it shows us the union of the Father and the Son in total harmony with the same love, the same objective, but yet different persons.

Therefore, through Jesus Christ we have the promise of a new and eternal covenant, established by the Father.

By which have been given to us exceedingly great and precious promises, that through these you may be partakers of the divine nature... 2^(nd) *Peter* 1:4

The promise of eternal life in the presence of God lives in all those who believe that God the Father sent His Son Jesus Christ to the world as an eternal sacrifice for the sins of humanity. Everyone who receives this sacrifice has passed over from eternal judgment to the grace and mercy of God. This great promise of God was given by the Father, delivered by the Son and sealed by the Holy Spirit.

"For God, (the Father) so loved the world that He gave His only begotten Son, that whoever believes in Him should not perish but have everlasting life." John 3:16

The word of God, from the Father is the words of truth. The Father has given His word to the Son and the Son has given the word to us, even in the times of the prophets of old. It has always been the Son, who is the mediator between the Father and us. The words of truth belongs to the Son just as much as they are the Father's, they are the word of God.

...Because My word has no place in you.

...Because you are not able to listen to My word.

...If anyone keeps My words he shall never see death.

John 8:37, 43, 51

These are the words of God, the Father and the Son, together with the Holy Spirit bringing forth the holy word of truth. For if we glorify the Son, we glorify the Father. If we pray to the Son, we pray to the Father. If we come before God the Father in the name of Jesus, we also come before Jesus.

Yet for us there is one God, the Father, of whom are all things, and we for Him; and one Lord Jesus Christ, through whom are all things, and through whom we live. 1ˢᵗ Corinthians 8: 6

This Scripture is clear in revealing that all God the Father has created, all that He has given to man has always been through the Son. This includes the promise to Abraham, the Law of Moses, and the Holy Spirit. We have never known the Father except through the Son, since the Scripture says, *through whom are all things.* Not some things, but all things come through the Son, and without the Son, God the Father gives nothing. Therefore, from the prophets of the law to the apostles of grace, it was the Son who was revealed to man, and through the Son, the Father is revealed since the two are in total union.

God the Father of whom are all things, the Lord Jesus Christ through whom are all things. God the Father has not, and will not reveal anything of His divine nature except through the Son, and the Son reveals Him. It is impossible to know the Father except through the Son, since the Scripture clearly says of the Son, *through whom are all things.* All things, all knowledge, all love and all life, comes through the Son from God the Father.

Jesus said to them, "If God were your Father, you would love Me, for I proceeded forth from God.

Good News

Have you ever heard someone say to you, "I have some good news?"

Most people have heard these words sometime in their lives. Maybe it was good news about a job promotion, maybe about test grades or maybe you won something, a gift you were not expecting. It could have been the good news about your health, or the health of a loved one. However, some people might question that in a time of rising expenses, rising crime and a rise in fatal diseases, what good news could come out of the world's troubled current events? The world is terrorized with the threats of evil from distant shores to our own local communities. Where is the good news, the hope of a better world, the hope of a better life?

The message of the early Christians was a proclamation of the Gospel (the Good News). The first church headed by the apostles, through God's careful direction, would proclaim the greatest news in the history of all creation. To the people of Israel, the coming of the Messiah was the greatest news they could ever hear. Israel's prophets had foretold this good news repeatedly, the coming of their King whose kingdom would see no end. What did Jesus Himself proclaim?

"The time has come", He said. "The Kingdom of God is near. Repent and believe the good news!"
Mark 1:15

The good news, the most wonderful, greatest news anyone could ever hear is that on an ordinary night, the supernatural move of God came, as the long awaited Savior, the Messiah, God's Son became a Man. The One, who all the prophets heard was coming; a King of all kings, who would save a lost and dying people, is finally here! On that night, God took on a human form and became one of us! Not born in a palace with servants, but born through a common woman in a small town. The Son of God, in whom all things were created through Him, makes a humble entrance into the human race. The years go by, and this baby grows into a Man, He waits and waits, and at the age of thirty, He then begins the work for which He came into the world. He reveals the very nature of the Creator to His creation. Then the time came for Him to complete another part of His mission, to bring the creation back to the Creator, the lost children back into the loving arms of their Father.

He would sacrifice Himself, as the Scripture says; *so that by the grace of God He might taste death for everyone.* Jesus conquered death to give us eternal life. That is the *good news,* the greatest news that we could ever hear! What does this really mean?

Jesus gave His life as a ransom for ours, for the debt of all our sins and on the third day, God raised Him up and now crowned Him with glory and honor forever; *His Kingdom will see no end,* and God has invited us to live with Him for eternity.

That is the best news I have ever heard. But wait, there is more! This life of eternity with God does not start when these bodies grow old and die, when there is a separation of our spirits from our physical bodies. This *good news* of eternal life with God can begin today! You see, once we accept the sacrifice of Jesus Christ as our payment for all our sins, our eternal life with God begins the moment we believe. So, how does this benefit us now?

I can tell you from my own experience, that once the burden of carrying my sin around was lifted from me:

Once I knew that I was no longer alone,

Once I knew that there is hope,

Once I started to believe God at His word,

Once I started to act on what God has already said,

The position of my heart began to change for the better!

Yes, the world is still plagued with evil acts of violence, greed, dishonesty, diseases, poverty and every act of sin against God and humanity that one could conceive. However, these are not in the Kingdom of God in which I am now a citizen. Moreover, the Kingdom of God can be the reality of your life today. Sound too good to be true? That is why God calls it the *good news!* Have you ever had someone ask you, 'I have good news and I have bad news, which one do you want first?' God tells us that He has some bad news, but He also has some very good news, the greatest news we could ever hear!

Bad news:

For all have sinned and fall short of the glory of God.

For the wages of sin is death…

Good news:

But the gift of God is eternal life in Christ Jesus our Lord.

That if you confess with your mouth the Lord Jesus and believe in your heart that God raised Him from the dead, you will be saved.

Romans 3: 23, 6: 23, 10: 9

The sacrifice of Jesus Christ was so perfect that by repenting from sin, believing it in your heart, and openly confessing this truth with your mouth, you have eternal life with God right now!

For with the heart one believes unto righteousness, and with the mouth confession is made unto salvation. For the Scripture says, "Whoever believes on Him (Jesus Christ), *will not be put to shame." For there is no distinction between Jew and Greek, for the same Lord over all is rich to all who call upon Him. For whoever calls on the name of the Lord shall be saved."*

Romans 10: 10 - 13

Jesus said to her, "I am the resurrection and the life; he that believes in Me, though he may die, he shall live. And whoever lives and believes in Me shall never die. Do you believe this?"

John 11: 25, 26

But God, who is rich in mercy, because of His great love with which He has loved us, even when we were dead in our trespasses, made us alive together with Christ (by grace you have been saved), and raised us up together in the heavenly places in Christ Jesus.

Ephesians 2: 4 - 6

Honest Scales

The Lord abhors dishonest scales, but accurate weights are His delight. Proverbs 11:1

God had granted King Solomon the gift of wisdom. God has given us all the Proverbs of King Solomon for our edification, to help us make wise decisions in this life. For the wisdom of God is one of the greatest gifts given to us that will help us through our human experience. They are to be used by us to build a life based on the foundation of God's principles in the Scriptures. I have found in my own life that by not building on God's foundation and trying to build on any other structure is defeating. Any other foundation, such as empty theories and philosophies are like building our lives on sand. They will simply not stand up to the storms of this life. Remember that God is faithful and true to His word. God cannot lie!

In the above Scripture God gives Solomon some insight when it comes to conducting business. God tells us that He *abhors dishonest scales*. The word *abhors* means to dislike intensely. Have you ever seen something that someone did and disliked it intensely? If you have, then you can relate to what God is saying when He sees someone cheating someone else in business. The scales are symbolic in keeping honest business practices in our day-to-day dealings. God dislikes intensely the practices of those who are not honest in business. Now I cannot speak for anyone else, but I want God to bless me and not turn away from me. If any of us thinks that God will bless someone who is conducting business in a way that God intensely dislikes, they should guess again. When anyone is doing something that God dislikes, acts against His word, it is sin. Moreover, with no repentance, they will reap the fruits of a sin. The principles of God are not just some old wives tales written for interesting reading. The principles of God are true and have been proven to work throughout the existence of humanity. We read in the next line that if we are honest, accurate in our business, God is pleased. Now again, if I am looking to please anybody, I want to please God. If I can please God, I know there is a good coming down the road for me by obeying His instruction. How can I make such a bold

statement? It is as I said before, God is faithful to His word and
His word says it repeatedly.
*A good man obtains favor from the Lord, but the Lord
condemns a crafty man. Proverbs 12:2,
He who seeks good finds goodwill, but evil comes to him who
searches for it. Proverbs 11:27*
God repeatedly tells us that if we plant poison mushroom
seeds, poison mushrooms will grow and not sweet tomatoes.
How can anyone think that if he or she does evil, evil will not
return to them? I believe God, because He says that if seeds of
dishonesty are planted, then a dishonest tree will grow. *What a
man sows he will reap.* I know there are times when we see
people who are dealing with dishonest scales and we wonder
why they are getting away with it. God makes it very clear, that
nobody gets away with anything. Someone might also ask, why
are there so many people that have become wealthy using
dishonest scales, lying and cheating in business? Why are they
still successful? God answers that question.
*The blessing of the Lord brings wealth and He adds no trouble
to it. Proverbs 10:22*
When God blesses you with wealth, He frees you from some of
the problems wealth can bring. We know that not all the money
in the world can buy us peace of mind or joy in our hearts. Not
all the diamonds and rubies can buy God given faith. These
things can only come from God alone. We can achieve many
goals in life, we can reach our objectives and strike the planned
targets, but without God's blessing, trouble will follow. Our
goals and objectives in this life should be to please God, to be
His delight not His abhorrence.
We should also consider how God has dealt with the men and
women in the Scriptures. We can see how God was angered,
and dealt with the hardhearted people of Israel. Even Samson,
who was deceived by the whispers of Delilah, found himself
bound and blind in a cell with little hope. Yet, God who is
merciful, answered his last prayer. I believe it hurt God to see
Samson in that state. Nevertheless, Samson decided to build
his house on sand instead of on the foundations of God. He
certainly reaped what he had sown. However, God is merciful

and forgives those who are willing to humble themselves before Him and repent. Repentance to God is not just saying I am sorry. It is a change in thinking to prevent us from repeating the same sin. No one said this was easy, but the results are worth any struggle.

Is it profitable to listen to God's direction? How can anyone ask that question? God is sovereign! In a second, He can read every thought of the entire population of the planet without a problem. Can we really comprehend the power of God? We cannot, but we can comprehend His principles, His promises, and His love for His creation called man. God knows us better than we know ourselves. He knows what will bring us trouble and what will save us from it. However, God does not take away our free will. He loves us too much for that, so God will allow us to make our mistakes. Samson and King David are two of the best examples of this. I believe it hurts God to watch His creation fall in error and reap the fruit of it, for we were not created to live in error. Now if we know the way of error, and do it anyway, this is sin.

Anyone, then, who knows the good he ought to do and does not do it, sins. James 4:17

God's principles are in order. His foundations of truth and justice are firmly set deep in all creation. However, He is a God of mercy, ready and willing to forgive all who humble themselves before Him.

Humble yourselves before the Lord and He will lift you up. *James 4:10*

God is waiting for us to realize that His way is the only way and apart from Him, there is no peace, no joy, and no life. God gives us a warning that this life will move by quickly before us. We look at the year on our calendars and ask, where did the months go? Our day is coming when we will stand before God, for this life is short and is quickly gone.

What is your life? You are a mist that appears for a little while and then vanishes. James 4:14

Fool on a Hill

*Do not deceive yourselves. If any one of you thinks He is wise
by the standards of age, he should become a fool so that he
may become wise. For the wisdom of this world is foolishness
in God's sight. 1 Corinthians 3:18-19*
Has the 20ᵗʰ century man gained so much independence that
he thinks he does not need God anymore? God says,
"Foolishness!" God also says, *"Do not deceive yourselves."* Is it
possible to deceive ourselves? God says that it is. How many
times in life, do we put on blinders on in certain situations and
only see what we want to see? How many times do we listen to
other people only to hear the part we want to hear instead of
really listening to the complete conversation? How many times
will we read a text, pick out what we like about it, and disregard
the rest? How many times do we totally disregard God?
God uses a key word when we leave Him out of our lives, and
the word is *foolishness.* That is why God says that if you think
that you are wise without the wisdom of God, you are a fool. It
would be better to become a fool concerning the so-called
wisdom that the world offers, and gain God's wisdom.
Hard concept to grasp? The knowledge of the things of this
world is temporary, but the knowledge and wisdom of God are
eternal.
God uses another key word and it is the word *deceives.* God
does not say that the devil will deceive us, He does not say that
another person will deceive us, He says, *"Do not deceive
yourselves."* For a person that deceives himself is a fool.
*Your commands make me wiser than my enemies, for they are
ever with me. I have more insight than all my teachers, for I
have more understanding than the elders, for I obey your
precepts. Psalm 119: 98-101*
Wisdom comes from the word of God. God's commands,
statutes, and precepts are all found in His written word. Do you
need a vision, a dream, or a revelation from God? We do not,
because we have God's word in writing, sealed by the Holy
Spirit of God. We have a written guarantee from God that not
only tells us right from wrong, but also tells us how much He
loves us. God explains to us that our spirits are the most

important part of our makeup. The spirit will live on long after our bodies give out and die.

The psalmist yields to the Spirit of God and tells us that the *wisdom of God will make us wiser than our enemies* and will give us more insight. Moreover, wisdom gives us understanding through obedience to the word of God. *Do not merely listen to the word and so deceive yourselves. Do what it says. James 1:22*

Again, we hear God say, *"Do not deceive yourselves."* Keep your heart open and listen to what the word of God says. For the person who hears the word of God and considers it foolishness is himself the fool. For who knows all things? God alone. In thinking that we do not need God, we are deceiving ourselves and are fools in every sense of the word. Do not deceive yourself by reasoning that God is not all knowing, the Almighty, the Creator and Sustainer of all things. Without God, there would be nothing because all things are in Him. God rules! *Do not deceive yourselves* by thinking that God is a small God who is limited to the logic and reasoning of man. God is a big God, who is far above man's thoughts. God, who needs only to speak a word and it is done, is supernatural, superior, and supreme. The truth is the truth; *do not deceive yourselves* in trading the truth for a lie, the truth for a theory, or the truth for a feeling. Whether you believe the truth or not, it remains the truth, even if it is rejected.

Jesus said to him, "I am the way, the truth and the life; no man comes to the Father but by Me." John 14: 6

Where is the wise man? Where is the scholar? Where is the philosopher of this age?

Has not God made foolish the wisdom of the world? For since in the wisdom of God the world through its wisdom did not know Him.... 1ˢᵗ Corinthians 1: 20-21

A Doorkeeper

Better is one day in your courts than a thousand elsewhere; I would rather be a doorkeeper in the House of my God than to dwell in the tents of the wicked. Psalm 84:10
God's wisdom shines through this verse like the sunlight that breaks through the clouds. One day in the presence of God would be more fulfilling than a thousand days out of His presence. After all, a thousand days without God would be a thousand empty days. God revealed to the psalmist that in the courts of His presence is by far the absolute best part of life. God is the Author of all life and to be in His presence is to be in the fullness of life. It is good to be in the presence of God, because that one-day, in His mighty presence is so energizing, it will carry us through a thousand days of trials.
I would rather be a Doorkeeper in the House of God. Psalm 84: 10
Here we begin to get an understanding on how God thinks. He puts in the heart of the psalmist, that all of us would be better off being a doorkeeper, (a door attendant) in the presence of God than some high position without Him. We would be better off doing the smallest task in His presence than some tremendous project without Him. God is trying to get through to us that the most important part of life is being with Him, in His presence. There are no earthly positions, accomplishments, goals, or targets that is more rewarding than living in communion with God. The smallest task that we can think of is so much greater with God, even greater than an enormous accomplishment without Him. Nothing that can be accomplished, no matter how huge it might seem, can compare to living in His presence. King David would have rather been a shepherd with God than a King without Him. David was saying, "I'll take the doorman position in God's presence than the president of a company or a country without Him." I would rather eat a plain bowl of rice in the presence of God than a seven course meal without Him. God wants us to have the best in life and of life, because God is the only Creator of all life. No one can give life except God. Man can build many things, but they are all dead materials without life. Think of

being in God's presence like being plugged into a life source. We are so used to just plugging something in to an electrical socket to make our lives easier. Cooking, cleaning, entertainment and on and on we could go. Our washing machines, our dishwasher, our TV's, all need a source of energy. All these things will work as long as they are plugged in. As the source of electricity that comes through the electrical lines in to our homes, so there is also a line called the source of life. He's God, the Creator of all life and we need to be plugged into Him! The psalmist writes that it is better to be plugged in with God, (Life's source), than to be unplugged and have no life. No connection (relationship), with God is a spiritual death. With no life in our spirits, we are just empty shells in a state of materialism, and self-indulgence. Better, is one day connected with God than a thousand days disconnected. Again, God is the source of all life.

Jesus answered; I am the way, the truth and the life.
John 14:6
Jesus answered the question that you may have been asking yourself as your reading this. How do I plug into God? Jesus makes this very clear.
No one comes to the Father except through Me. John 14:6
Jesus teaches us that He is the only way to be plugged into life's source. Jesus is the power line, but he is also the power. He is the way to God, and He is the life source. God the Father has given all that to Him. If we are plugged into Jesus, we are plugged into the God the Father. If we receive Jesus, we receive the Father. If we are connected to Jesus, we are connected to God the Father, Son, and Holy Spirit. When connected, plugged in, we are energized with life, by the source of all life, who is God. We are fused with His Spirit, the Holy Spirit and His life runs through us like electrical power through a wire. However, disconnected or unplugged, we are then in a spiritual death. Like the machine, that has no power source.
The existence without God might look good, but it is dead, so it no longer has a purpose. It is lacking the source that enables it to do what it was created to do, live in the presence of God.

Nevertheless, when the power source is connected, it is useful and can be used for the purpose it was created. Our purpose and very reason for being is to know God. Moreover, once we know Him, we are connected, and become energized, filled with life, love, and mercy because that is who God is. Without God, we are just empty and shallow shells. Now the psalmist says that He would *rather be a doorkeeper*, a person whose responsibility is to stand by the door. We have seen this in many big hotels in large cities. You might say to yourself, 'not a very impressive job.' Well, the doorkeeper is like a servant, like a butler or a house cleaner. God says that we are better off a doorkeeper with Him than a doctor, a lawyer, a president, or a king without Him. This leads into another truth that is a misunderstanding even among some of us. God is not saying that He does not want us to have a higher education and things that we need in this life. Like any good parent, God wants His children to have what is best for them. However, let us take a step out of the natural and into the spiritual world. Any true believer is a doorkeeper, a person who holds the door open for all people whom God calls to come in. What greater position is there in the spiritual for a believer? If we think of our witnessing as opening the door to heaven, then I can not think of a more important role in the entire universe. This is the highest form of praise and worship we can give God. When we are willing to be a doorkeeper for Him, and invite others into the Lord's mercy, we are showing God how much we love Him, trust Him, and honor Him as the one and only God.

Revelation 3:20
Behold, I stand at the door and knock. If anyone hears My voice and opens the door, I will come in to him...

Honor

The meaning of honor is to respect the personal integrity of a person, a high regard for someone. God agrees with this definition. God tells us to hold certain people in honor.

Honor and thanks to Him who sits on the throne and who lives forever and ever.... Revelation 4:9

Honor your father and mother.... Matthew 19:19

Honor the Lord with your wealth.... Proverbs 3:9

Marriage should be honored by all.... Hebrews 13:4

The insight to honor is that by respecting your father and mother, by faithfulness in the marriage covenant and by obeying the Lord with your heart, we can show God by our actions how much we love Him. By honoring what God says, we honor Him by following His commands. Moreover, by doing good instead of evil, we show that we hold a high regard for His integrity. We are simply not only telling God, but also showing Him by our deeds that we respect Him and honor Him as God. God shows us that there are many people who say they honor Him with words, but not in their actions.
These people come near to Me with their mouth and honor Me with their lips, but their hearts are far away from Me. Isaiah 29:13
To respect your parents, to respect your marriage, and to respect what God has entrusted you with; all bring honor and glory to God. This honor is worship unto the Lord. Jesus quotes the above text in Matthew 15:8, when He shouts at the Pharisees, *"You hypocrites!"* Is not a hypocrite someone who says one thing and does another? God says that if you want to honor Him, honor Him by your words and actions. It is only when we honor God with our speech and our actions that God will honor us.

Jesus said:
"My Father will honor the one who serves Me."
John 12:26
By honoring your parents, by honoring your marriage, by honoring the Lord with what He has entrusted you with, you are serving Jesus Christ. Not all are called to a foreign mission field, not all are called to be a leader in the church. Not all are called to write or sing in the will of God. But all are called to serve the Lord by honoring those who He honors. God never asks us to do something that He Himself is unwilling to do.
Those who honor Me I will honor, but those who despise Me will be disdained.
1ˢᵗ Samuel 2:30
We can be sure that God is faithful and will keep His promise; so let us honor God by the way we live. Not as though we are earning points and with enough points, we will be allowed to live in heaven when we leave here. We can honor God because of what He has already done. He has given us the gift of eternal life through His Son Jesus Christ. We can honor the Lord our God because we know that every word He has spoken is true. Moreover, living in the will of God is the greatest honor for us. For God's glory reaches beyond the galaxies, beyond our imaginations, and certainly above our way of thinking. He is God, who is ageless, limitless, all knowing, all-powerful, and is all love. His throne is above the heavens, yet His love has touched the earth. Whom else can we honor as God? No one else is worthy, because God alone is worthy of all our praise and all our worship. Now this is the wisdom that is above all knowledge, all mysteries and theologies, is to honor God with every word and deed, honor Him by our lives. Let God look down from His throne and know that He is loved by the way He is honored, as we present our lives as glory to Him.
I beseech you brethren, by the mercies of God, that you present your bodies as a living sacrifice, holy, acceptable to God, which is your reasonable service.
Romans 12: 1

The Potato

He who forgives an offense seeks love...
Proverbs 17:9

A teacher once told each of her students to bring a clear plastic bag and a sack of potatoes to class. She then instructed the students to write on each potato the name of someone who they had never really forgiven, and place the potato in the plastic bag. Some of the students had quite a load of potatoes in their bag. The teacher then instructed the students to take the bag of potatoes home from class and do not return to class without them for one week.

After three days of lugging the potatoes back and forth to class, the students began to complain, argue among themselves, and become very negative about the hardship of carrying the weight of the potatoes. The students also became very negative against the teacher who had instructed such a senseless assignment. It was not long before the students figured out that if they could only get rid of these sacks of potatoes, their complaining, arguing and negativity would stop and would even enjoy the class and the teacher as they did before the assignment had started. Then the teacher simply explained to them to forgive each person whose name was written on the potato and then throw the potato out. The choice was theirs to either forgive the person whose name was written on the potato and be free from the weight of lugging it around; or hold on to the potato, hold on to the pain of carrying that thing around. The teacher told them, 'the choice is yours.'

'...But if you do not forgive men their trespasses, neither will your heavenly Father forgive your trespasses.
Matt. 6:15

When we carry the weight of not forgiving in our hearts, the results are complaining, arguing, and negativity with those around us. There can be no freedom from bitterness, no peace of mind without forgiveness. It is not easy to forgive a person who has committed a wrong against you or your love ones. However, whether we realize it or not, we are the ones that will carry the weight of bitterness in our hearts. Does the resistance of not forgiving someone really turn into bitterness? Speak to any bitter person you know and listen to them talk. It will not take long before you find that the seed of unforgiving has taken root in their hearts and has grown into a vine of negativity and resentment. This vine will grow around our hearts and choke the joy of living out of our lives. Moreover, that sack of potatoes, the load of carrying the weight of remorse will wear us down until we are completely blind to the root of the problem. This is not to say that crimes against humanity should not be brought to justice. The Scriptures tells us that authorities have been set in place for that very purpose, because God is the final Judge, and He will execute true justice according to His wisdom. However, as for us, God teaches us to forgive and God will do the rest. This is by far the hardest lesson given by Christ to accept and to practice, but there is a price to pay if we resist this truth, even in these physical bodies, as our minds are tortured from resentment, which causes physical disorder.

Jesus promised freedom from resentment, hatred, contentions, jealousies and revelries. For these things are a curse from sin, but in Christ we are free from the curse, because Jesus Himself took the curse on His own body and nailed it to a tree.

The choice is ours, we can keep carrying that sack of resentment and hatred, or we can be free from it, letting it go and move forward into the kingdom of God.

If the Son sets you free, you will be free indeed.
John 8:3
Christ has redeemed us from the curse of the law, having become a curse for us (for it is written), "Cursed is everyone who hangs on a tree"), that the blessing of Abraham might come upon the Gentiles in Jesus Christ, that we might receive the promise of the Spirit through faith.
Galatians 3: 13, 14
"Should you not also have had compassion on your fellow servant, just as I had pity on you?"
Matthew 18: 33

The Potter

The word which came to Jeremiah from the Lord, saying, "Arise and go down to the potter's house, and there I will cause you to hear my word." Then I went down to the potter's house, and there he was making something at the wheel. In addition, the vessel that he made of clay was marred in the hand of the potter, so he made it again into another vessel, as it seemed good to the potter.
Jeremiah 18:1 - 4

God spoke to the heart of Jeremiah and told him that there was something of great value going on in the house of a person who made cups, bowls and plates out of clay. So, Jeremiah goes to the potter's house, and we are invited along with him to learn what the potter is making. When Jeremiah arrives at the potter's house, he sees the potter at the wheel, a spinning stand that rotates so the clay can be molded. Now God calls this lump of clay that was being molded into some kind of cup or bowl, *a vessel*. A *vessel* is used to hold something inside of it and transport it from one place to another. A cup or a bowl is used to transport food and drink from the container, into your mouth. While Jeremiah was watching, the potter spins the clay and molds it by the pressing of his hands, but something happened to the clay. God tells us that it was marred in the hands of the potter. A defect in the clay was discovered that caused the cup or bowl that was to be shaped, to be damaged. Maybe a small stone was imbedded in the clay that caused a scourged line to rip across the vessel. Whatever it was, it caused the object to be defected. Who would buy such a cup or bowl with a scratch through its surface? The piece would be worthless. So, the potter, who still has the same lump of partially formed clay on the wheel, removes the defect and makes another vessel from the same lump of clay. God reminds us that the potter made the choice to make the clay into a new vessel, which means the potter started from the beginning, spinning the same clay, but this time without the defect, and it becomes a new vessel, defect free. When the potter is completely satisfied with the final shape of the clay, then it can be used for its intended purpose. The potter did not make the vessel just to be viewed, but to be used as a container to transport something good such as food or drink. Can the vessel, a lump of clay, be used for an intended purpose before the potter molds it? No, a lump of clay without the proper shape will not be able to hold or transport anything. It is useless in its present form. Without the molding of the potter's hand, it is just a lump of clay with no purpose. Was God showing Jeremiah and us that we are the lumps of clay and He is the Potter? Yes, but He is showing us much more than that. There is a purpose for the clay and a purpose for us. The clay is shaped and molded into a vessel that can be useful. We are also vessels to be formed by God, to be used by removing the defect (sin), and filling us with His Holy Spirit. Once we are filled, we can be used to transport the Spirit of God to other vessels, other people. What greater purpose can there be than being God's cup to feed the lost, hungry people who do not even realize that they are in a state of spiritual starvation. Before any person can be used for the greatest purpose in all existence, like the lump of clay, we must first become molded, transformed and changed from a vessel that has no form to hold anything of great value, to a form that can carry the living Spirit of God. Like the cup or the bowl, we also need to be shaped, by the empting of self, to create a cavity, a space that will accept the Spirit of God inside of us. The lump of clay with no cavity is simply full of its own substance. God is in the process of molding us in a shape that will create a cavity, an empty place where the Spirit of God can fill us. With most of us, like the lump of clay, we are simply full of ourselves, there is no room for God to enter and fill us. We have a solid form that is full of selfish ambitions. There is no inner surface, just an outer surface. As the lump of clay, we have no inner place, no form to hold and transport anything except for sin, and most important, we have no real purpose. We have been robbed of the highest position of purpose in all creation; the purpose of transporting the Holy Spirit, His love and His mercy to one another.

In some cases, the clay has been formed into a cup or bowl, but the empty space has been filled with greed, lust, resentment, and fear, causing the vessel to be marred and used for evil instead of good. God shows us something else in the potter's house that should influence our thinking. The clay that was on the potter's wheel was in some way defective. God tells us that the potter, using the same clay, made another vessel, a new vessel. The small stick or stone that entered the human heart is sin. Sin is the defect, the only factor that will prevent us from molding into the correct form so we can be used for our intended purpose. It may not always be the most prominent sins like murder, adultery, or stealing. As we know, there can be lust in someone's heart without even committing the act. It could be the sin of envy, the sin of resentment, the sin of unforgiving or the sin of pride. Whatever that defect is, God says that He is as the potter. He is more than able to remove the defect. This is the most important fact about the power of God concerning His ability to change our lives in a new birth, a transformation into a new creature. God asks Jeremiah this very important question:

"O house of Israel, can I not do with you as this potter?" says the Lord. "Look, as the clay is in the potter's hands, so are you in my hand, O house of Israel!"
Jeremiah 18:6

Was this lesson only for the house of Israel? Why not ask the question this way, O church of Jesus Christ; can I not do with you as this potter? Are we not in God's hands? God can make us into vessels with an eternal purpose; vessels of honor and truth, vessels that can be used by God to save the lost, heal the sick, and bring forth a harvest of faith.

Does not the potter have power over the clay...?
But now, O Lord, you are our Father, we are the clay, and you are the potter, and we are all the work of your hand.
Romans 9:21, Isaiah 64:8

Victory by Faith

...For everyone born of God overcomes the world. This is the victory that has overcome the world, even our faith.
1ˢᵗ John 5:4

God promises us a victory over the world (man's system of governing according to his own fallen nature), by using one of the most powerful weapon in the arsenal of God. The weapon is faith in the living promises (word), of God, who is Jesus Christ. To have a true victory, a true faith is required. A victimized attitude will not produce victory. Complaining and grumbling will not produce victory. Faith is positive not negative.

"...If you have faith as small as a mustard seed.... Nothing will be impossible for you."
Matthew 17:20

Listen to what God is saying. Just a little faith, the size of a small seed will produce victory; it will bring the power of God into our lives. Do not under estimate that little seed of faith. Planted in the right soil, it will grow into a massive tree. Once the young tree is deeply rooted, it becomes a tree that bears fruit, a tree that is not easily moved. Plant that seed of faith in a child and you will see how deeply rooted he or she becomes.

Faith that is planted and watered will grow by hearing the word of God, and then surrendering to it in the power of word and deed will produce victory. Do you want a faith that produces victory? God's word is the only way; they are the very thoughts of God that expresses Himself in every page of Scripture. Without faith in His word, there is no victory. God has given us the super high-test fuel to skyrocket our faith so we can live above this world instead of being defeated by evil. We can fly on the wings of the Spirit of God. *In the world, but not of the world.* Soaring above the storms of this life, because we know that God is faithful! In God is our faith, not faith in our place of occupation, or faith in man's so-called knowledge. If we are willing to trust God, God will show us every time how faithful and merciful He is. If God said it, you can trust that God will come through on every promise. God's word will produce faith, faith will produce victory and victory will give freedom from the sin that so eagerly wants to steal the hope that has been bought and paid for by the blood of our Savior Jesus Christ. Faith moves the hand of God and no enemy can stand against Him. It is God's good pleasure, His mercy and out of His great love, that He has called us His children. Therefore, God being our Father, who is faithful in love, protects those who love Him. There is only one word that should be used in describing a lifetime of running in the faith in the living God, and that word is victory!

"I saw Satan fall like lightning from heaven."
Luke 10:18

God's word will transform us from a world of defeat, sorrow and death; to His kingdom of joy, victory and eternal life. Once the word of God becomes our reference, our influence on how to live, then the mercy of God will shower us like a summer down pour rain. Trust Jesus Christ, because He has already overcome the world, He is victorious!

"Behold, My Servant whom I have chosen, My Beloved in whom My soul is well pleased! I will put My Spirit upon Him, and He will declare justice to the Gentiles. He will not quarrel nor cry out, nor will anyone hear His voice in the streets, a bruised reed He will not break, a smoking flax He will not quench, till He sends forth justice to victory; And in His name the Gentiles will trust."
Matthew 12 18 – 21

Victory is ours by trusting, believing, which is faith in the name, which is above every name, which is the only name that men can be saved. It is the name of our Savior, our Lord, our Redeemer, our Sacrifice; God the Son, that can bring victory to every area of our lives. No matter how hopeless things may appear, if we are in Him, then we have victory! Because, every knee, whether on earth, under the earth, or in heaven; every knee, not just some knees, will bend, or break before the King of all kings, Jesus the Christ, who was, who is, and will always be. In His name, we have faith to the glory of God!

Something Happened

Once you were alienated from God and were enemies in your minds because of your evil behavior. But now He has reconciled you by Christ's physical body through death...
Colossians 1:21 & 23
But now in Christ Jesus you who once were far away have been brought near through the blood of Christ.
Ephesians 2:13
The above Scriptures are the testimonies of every Christian who has had an encounter with God. The key words in these Scriptures are *alienated* and *far away*. God tells us that it is very possible to be *alienated* from Him. Have you ever been *alienated* from anyone in your life? When we are *alienated* from someone, the first thing to be disconnected is communication. As the communication becomes less and less, the parties will drift apart. That can happen in any relationship. At times, these people can become so far apart that they can even become enemies. If it has never happened to you, you should thank God, but if it has, then you can get an idea of what God is saying. *Alienated* means; to be separated from another person, or persons. God tells us that we are separated from Him unless something happens. In both Scriptures the words, *"but now"* meaning something changed. The change took place because of a rescue mission from God, and He calls it *redemption.*
For He rescued us from the dominion of darkness and brought us into the kingdom of His Son whom He loves, in whom we have redemption, the forgiveness of sins.
Colossians 1:13& 14
I like that word *rescue,* because when you need to be rescued, you have to rely on the one who is rescuing and not something you could have done yourself. If you could have done it yourself, you would not need to be rescued. When I hear the word *rescue,* I think of someone helpless, drowning, sinking, lost, ship wrecked, broken, crushed, and unable to find a way out, and then come a hero to the *rescue.* Well most people will say, I do not need to be rescued, I am a good person, and I even go to church, I am not drowning.

Most people think that as long as they are not physically ill and they have some money in the bank, or as long as they are working, everything is fine between them and God. This could not be further from the truth. If your body is healthy and so is your bank account, without God you could still be incomplete and *alienated* from eternal life. We consistently attempt to fill our lives with all the world has to offer. Money being the first, our jobs, our entertainment, our sports, our families, our relationships, material things, hobbies, clubs, food, and any other pleasures we can think of including the state of the art information systems. Yet, ask most people how they are doing and you will hear nothing but complaints.

My question to them is if you have all these things, then why are you still complaining? The answer is an empty heart; God is not there. Most people will never admit that there is something missing in their lives. However, some will admit it by saying they just feel empty. Now when the Apostle Paul was writing to the churches in Ephesus, and Corinth by the Spirit of God, he was addressing people who once had the same problem, that empty feeling caused by an empty heart. God had reminded them, and is also showing us, that all of us were *alienated* from Him at one point in time. However, something happened; something made them change. Something made them make peace with God and open their hearts toward Him. That something is someone, and His name is Jesus Christ. The people in that day, who were just as empty as any one of us, believed the eternal truth that Jesus Christ is the Son of God and that He died on the cross for our sins, and was raised from the dead in glory.

God made you alive with Christ. He forgave us all our sins, having canceled the written code, with it regulations, that was against us and that stood opposed to us; He took it away nailing it to the cross.
Colossians 2:13

The something that happened was a re-birth into a living hope, not an organized group of people that some call a belief, but a relationship with the living eternal God. They received the truth of the Gospel of Jesus Christ and believed, not because of how self-righteous they were, but because they were willing to open their hearts to God. They were willing to trust God. Now think about this for one moment. If you have many things that the world has to offer, but you are, just plain empty with whatever you have and what you are doing in your life, what could you possibly have to lose by trusting God?

All the houses, cars, hobbies, memberships, relationships or anything else that this world can offer equals to zero compared to the wisdom and knowledge of eternal life in Jesus Christ. Something happened to the people in those cities that the Apostle Paul was compelled to write about. That something has happened repeatedly for the last two thousand years. That something is called a re-birth of the spirit.

"That which is born of the flesh is flesh, and that which is born of the Spirit is spirit. Do not marvel that I said to you, 'You must be born again.'"
John 3: 6, 7

The people in the days of the Apostle Paul had the same sin and the same problems that we have today. Due to the state of high technology, we think of ourselves as more advanced, but we still have the same crimes, the same sin, and still resist the extended hand of God. However, something happened to the people, and that something is Jesus Christ coming into their hearts and changing them, forgiving their sins that had weighed them down for so many years. This gift of salvation, given by God and not earned through merit for the works of good deeds, is here and available today for all those who are willing to receive it. It is the Good News of God's promise that had been proclaimed by the prophets of old and has now come to pass. Today is the day of salvation; His offer still stands as it did in the days of the Apostle Paul. God has not changed His plan of hope. He is waiting for all to come to Him to receive the forgiveness of sin through the power of the sacrifice of Jesus Christ.

Sing to the Lord, all the earth; proclaim the good news of His Salvation from day to day. Declare His glory among the nations, His wonders among the people.
1st Chronicles 16:23 & 24

In His Merciful Love

Therefore, be imitators of God as dear children. And walk in love, as Christ also loved us and gave Himself for us as an offering and a sacrifice to God for a sweet aroma.
Ephesians 5: 1& 2
As a young boy will try to imitate his father, or a young girl attempts to imitate her mother, God tells us to be imitators of Him. When first reading the above Scripture we might say to ourselves, 'how can I imitate God?' I have all these faults, I am not perfect, I have times of anger, my feelings get hurt, and I lose my temper. How could I imitate God who is perfect, holy, and all knowing? God says there is a way, although it will not be easy at first, but we can do it. Would God command us to do something that is beyond our reach? No! If we choose to be imitators of God, if we walk in His light of truth, we need to be willing to walk in love. For there is one gift that God has given to everyone, and that gift is the power to love!

If I speak in tongues of men and angels.... If I have the gift of prophecy and can fathom all mysteries...and if I have faith that can move mountains...If I give all I posses to the poor and surrender my body to flames, but have not love, I gain nothing.
1ˢᵗ Corinthians 13:1 - 3
What a powerful revelation given to the Apostle Paul on the greatest gift given to man. Not all of us have gifts of prophecy, teaching, healing, or other miraculous powers. But the greatest gift, the one that God says is more important than even the gift of healing, is a gift that each and every one of us possess. That gift is the power to love.
It is funny how some of us seek the less important gifts in life and overlook the greatest gift we already have. God reveals to the Apostle Paul that without acting in the gift of love, all the other gifts amount to zero. After all, Jesus Christ is the full manifestation of God's love. God, who gives all good things as gifts to all people, has given us the ability to love. Is it easy? It should be since we already posses it. God also gives us so many other gifts. He gives us houses and cars, food and drink, and anything that is useful in this life. Out of all the things we

strive to have, God says to place them far behind the greatest power that He has given us, the power to love. For if we owned all the houses, cars, clothes and any other possession we could think of, and have never used the greatest gift of all, we have gained nothing, and we amount to nothing. Think about what God is telling us. He is actually showing us how He defines our measure of success. God is saying that we can even rule countries, yet if we have not love we are unsuccessful in His eyes.

Why do we place such a high regard on what our definition of success is, yet we turn a deaf ear to what God tells us is true success. It is sad that with all our accomplishments we hold up as great, God says they are nothing without love. So why is there such an absence of love in the world today? Why is there so much confusion and so many evil practices?

For where you have envy and selfish ambitions, there you will find disorder and every evil practice. James 3:16

Hear the word of God. He tells us that *envy and selfish ambitions* cause *disorder* and confusion. It is like someone who is walking in the dark, banging and bumping along his or her way. God goes one-step further to explain that out of envy and selflessness will grow every other type of evil practices. The root of the problem begins with the acts of *envy and selfish ambition,* and these can so easily entrap us and will blind us from the light of God's love and mercy.

So what can we do? What hope do we have? We have the greatest hope in all creation. The only thing we need to do is follow the life of Jesus Christ. One-step at a time and we can learn to live in the love of God. It might sound farfetched, but God says that we can do it with His power in us!

But the wisdom that comes from heaven is first of all pure, then peace loving, considerate, submissive, full of mercy and good fruit, impartial and sincere.

James 3: 17

Here God gives us a systematic instruction on how to walk in His love. If we can learn to live in God's word, then our lives will be full, not only with the love of God, but also with His wisdom. To walk in the love of God is by far the wisest thing anyone could ever do! God explains that if we plant the seed of mercy, if we plant the seed of consideration, if we plant the seed of peace, we will reap a harvest of righteousness. For where the righteousness of God is, so will be His blessings. God does not give *disorder* and confusion. We do that all by ourselves in choosing to walk in darkness, or should I say stumble in darkness, rather than running in the light of God's love.

Are we able to imitate God, even with all our faults? Can we give thanks instead of complaints? Can we bless someone instead of cursing them? Can we give rather than only take? Can we love instead of hate? There is no question about it, if we have His mercy in us; we are more than able to choose love over hate. The real question is do we really want to choose forgiveness over resentment, peace over war. Do we enjoy complaining, envy, and the fight to have things our way? God tells us that there is another way, a lighted path that leads to divine love.

I say then: Walk in the spirit and you shall not fulfill the lust of the flesh.

Galatians 5:16

When someone would say to me that they were walking in the spirit, I use to think to myself that they had some high calling from God. That they somehow tapped into a spiritual well that would aid them in every move and every word in their lives.

We do have a spiritual Helper, the Holy Spirit, who does guide us, but there is no secret, some floating on a cloud or some carefree existence that defines us as spiritual. The fact of the matter is that being a spiritual person really means obeying the word of God.

Just remember the objective of our enemy, Satan. He wants to cause us to fall in our relationship with God. His goal is to sow into us hate, envy, and pride. Those thought patterns lead us deeper and deeper into sin. If he can convince us of his lies, then he can use us to hurt other people, even people that we confess to love. After all, where do you think those people who hurt you got their advice?

God tells us that living in the knowledge of His love will bring us closer and closer in union with Him. When we begin to learn from God, we begin to learn more about His nature, which is something that no one can fully comprehend. Nevertheless, this we do know:

God is Love.
Love never fails.
1st John 4:16, 1st Corinthians 13:8
So if love never fails, God never fails and we are running in His love, we can never fail, not because of how great we are, but because how great God is.
Now these remain faith, hope, and love. But the greatest of these is love. 1st Corinthians 13:13
But because of His great love for us, God, who is rich in mercy, made us alive in Christ even when we were dead in transgressions. It is by grace you have been saved.
Ephesians 2:4
God's love for us is great and rich in mercy. His love invites us to come to Him just the way we are. God is willing to accept us with all our problems, all of our hang-ups (pride, greed, and selfishness) and all our faults, but loves us too much to keep us that way. He only asks that we trust Him.
"If you love Me, keep My commandments." John 14:15
Jesus focuses on a relationship between God and us. You cannot really love somebody unless you have a relationship with him or her. Jesus is telling us that if we have a relationship with Him, a love relationship, then obeying His commandments will be more natural than breaking them. So is the Christian life a walk of commandments? The Christian life is a run in the mercy and love of God that is based on our relationship with Him.
"I am the true vine and My Father is the gardener. He cuts off every branch in Me that bears no fruit, while every branch that does bear fruit He prunes so that it will be even more fruitful." John 15:1
Is it easy? No, but as the learning process develops, as we build a deeper understanding of Christ, each step of faith begins to be easier. Jesus tells us that we can do it. With every step and with every leap of faith, we can run with the love and mercy of God.

His Love

Give thanks to the Lord, for He is good; His love endures forever.
For God so loved the world that He gave His only begotten Son that whosoever believes in Him should not perish but have everlasting life.
Psalm 107:1, John 3:16

God's love endures forever. But how can we really understand God if we do not understand love? God's very nature is love. Do we really know what love means? I hear people say that they love their cars, they loved the movie they just watched, they love their houses, they love to eat, and of course, they will say in the same breath, 'I love my family.' We throw the word love around like a paper towel. Do we know what love is? When I looked up the word love in Webster's Dictionary, I was disappointed to read the definition as follows: Love, a strong feeling of attraction resulting from sexual desire. Is that how we want to define the word love to the next generation? That is not love, that is lust! Love is not just a feeling! It is no wonder we cannot understand God, look at what we think of His very nature. Love is not an attraction resulting from sexual desire. Love is an action of forgiving, and giving; love is an action of putting the one you say you love first.

God explains what love is:

Love is patient, love is kind. It does not envy, it does not boast, it is not proud. It is not rude, it is not self-seeking. It is not easily angered; it keeps no records of wrongs.
1st Corinthians 13:4 & 5

Love is not self-seeking. Do we love someone because it feels good? If anyone of us says we love someone, we should be willing to put that person first. If we say we love someone and still say to ourselves, 'I am first,' then we are fooling ourselves. If we say we love God but are not willing to put Him first, then we are telling God that we really love ourselves more. So how can we understand God if we cannot comprehend His very nature?

God tells us that His love for us endures forever. Now remember what love is, love is not self-seeking. God does not love us because it makes Him feel good, God does not love us because He wants something from us. God certainly does not love us because of how great we think we are. God did not ask our permission to love us. God loves us because of who He is, and not what we are. God is patient, God is kind, God does not envy, and God does not boast, God is not proud, God is not rude or self-seeking. God is love. If we can understand what love is, we can understand something of God, because love is His very nature, and then we can understand how much He loves us. God loves us so much that He was willing to become one of us and pay the price for our sins.

When Jesus was seen after His death and resurrection, we can eavesdrop on the conversation between the Lord and Thomas. *Then He said to Thomas, "Put your fingers here; See my hands. Reach out your hand and put it in My side. Stop doubting and believe."*

John 20:27

Jesus today is saying the same words to you and I. 'Look at the holes in My hands and feet, look at the hole in My side. I let this happen to Me for one reason, because I love you. I was willing to take your punishment for your sins.'

Now that is love! In the above text we can try to comprehend the sacrifice God was willing to make for us. He was willing to send His Son from a place that we can not even imagine, to sinful earth. He humbled Himself to become a mortal man, and then to be beaten and killed for one reason. The reason is when you love someone; you are willing to put him or her first. God was willing to put us first, therefore, why cannot we do the same for Him.

Love is not self-seeking. So if you want to know how much God loves you, just close your eyes and in the movie house of your minds, picture our Lord Jesus standing in front of you with the holes that are still in His hands, feet and side that says, 'I love you.'

Prayer

Then He taught, saying to them, "Is it not written, My house shall be called a house of prayer for all nations?"
Mark 11:17

In the age of microwave information, blasting through cable lines across the Internet, I am afraid we lose sight of the most powerful information ever given to man. Faster than a speeding bullet, more powerful than a locomotive, more informative than any Internet. I am talking about the power of prayer. Many people have many opinions on prayer. Well, they could be right on some points, but God is still the authority on the subject. Is prayer just a bunch of repeated words that we say, as if God does not understand what we are saying? Don't be silly! God knew what we were about to say before the foundation of the world. So why does religion teach us to repeat the same words, as if we sound like a recording. I cannot speak for religion, but I can tell you what Jesus taught about the subject of prayer.

In addition, when you pray, do not use vain repetitions as the heathen do. For they think that they will be heard for their many words." Matthew 6:7

So is prayer just a repetitive exercise of saying the same thing? Jesus said that people who do that, do it in vain. They are wasting their breath because the words are coming from the head and not the heart. Jesus warns us not to pray like that, but He gives us clear instructions on how to pray from the heart.

But you, when you pray, go into your room, and when you have shut your door, pray to your Father who is in the secret place...
Matthew 6:6

Jesus is telling us about a secret place, a place of prayer, a communion of communication with God, a place of heart where we can fellowship with Divinity. The place is in His presence. Think about it, we can have an appointment with God without telephones calls and sitting in a waiting room for hours. We can plug into the promises of God at anytime, day or night, walk-ins are welcome, and no appointments are necessary. We do not have to call someone else to book us a flight into His presence. We have the official travel agent of God, the Holy Spirit, who in seconds can take us before the throne of grace. Need a vacation from the world? Start praying. God tells us that by our prayers in faith we can move His hand. Once God begins to move in our lives, things will start changing, all for the better. Jesus teaches us about private time with God, a moment of just Him and you alone, and He is listening. Jesus tells us the results of the intimate prayer.

...And your Father who sees in secret will reward you openly. Matthew 11:6

Prayers get results! Worrying, wondering, fearing does not, except for the damage it does to our nerves. When we learn to trust God with the things we cannot change, things will begin to change for the better. So many times in my life, I have given my problems to God only when I have tried my plan "A", plan "B", all the way to "Z" with no real success. What I mean by no real success is, I seemed to solve the problem now, but it just showed up in somebody or at some place else later. The reason why that happens is that there are issues that we have, and God wants to deal with those issues. God does not band-aide problems as we do. God wants to plant His word in rich soil, so He sifts out the weeds. These weeds are some of the things, like past hurts that we carry around with us. God wants to fix our problems permanently. One of the best times for God to do His work is during our prayers. Even when we are praying for someone else, God is working on our hearts. Throughout the Scriptures, we have examples of how men and women who believed God prayed with life changing results. Remember whom it is we are praying to. Think about the awesome power and size of His creation, the temperature of the sun, the distance of the universe, the winds, and the sea of the earth. Now, think for a moment about the Creator who created all these things. We are not praying to some empty belief, we are praying to God who the Scriptures tell us that we are made in *His image and likeness.* We are praying to the one and only God who not only created all things, but also controls all things. Somehow, we have come up with the notion that God created the universe and then just let it go out of control. That is the farthest thing from the truth. The universe and all that is in it is governed by the word of God. The only ones that do not seem to realize this are us! The sun, the moon, the stars, the earth and all that is on the earth except for man, and a group of fallen angels are in the will of God. Therefore, when we do realize that God is in complete control, our prayer life will become firmly rooted in faith.

Now faith believes the things unseen. Abraham, Moses, David and through the apostles, all prayed prayers of faith. All of them knew that God is more than able to intervene in their lives and change their circumstances. The real question is whether we are willing to believe that God can and will change us in the process, and then our circumstances can also change. Are we willing to trust God? Sounds like a silly question. Most people will say, 'of course I trust God.' Well, if we do trust Him, then why do we worry so much? Why do we look at our problems, give them to God and then seconds later take them back and search for our own solutions? If we pray a prayer of faith, God cannot resist; He will act on that prayer if it is according to His will and His mercy.

The effective, fervent prayer of righteous man avails much. James 5:15

The effective prayer is the prayer that is prayed in faith according to the principles of God. If we only pray for our selfish wants and ambitions then we do it in vain. God would actually be doing us an injustice if we went crying to Him for only selfish wants. However, if we go before Him with our worship, our needs, and the needs of others in faith, things will happen.

Therefore, I tell you, whatever you ask for in prayer, believe that you have received it, and it will be yours. Mark 11:24

Think just for another moment about God. I mean stop, do not let any other thought, distraction, or any other voice disturb you for just a minute. God is in love with us. I know this is hard to believe, but it is true. When He looks into our eyes, it is like the new mother looking at her infant. Even that example falls short of explaining the love God has for us. Now think for a moment how we act or have acted when we were in love. All the ones we love, whether a spouse, child, parent or sibling are forever in our hearts, and in our minds. Their faces are forever before us. If they asked us for help, we would be there in a heartbeat to help them. Therefore, we know that we are capable of responding in love. Now think again about God. God is pure love. There is no impurity, no faults, and no defects, in His love. Think about when He looks in our eyes when we are asking Him for help. I tell you that our God will move mountains, bring down walls, and part waters for the ones who look up to Him for help in faith. The Apostle Paul, a mighty prayer warrior, prays a prayer to the church that hits the bulls-eye with living a life of prayer.

I pray also that the eyes of your understanding being enlightened in order that you may know the hope to which He has called you... Ephesians 1:18

Knowing how to pray is a result of understanding that we are in Christ. We were called, all that believe, with the ability, a gift, a direct line to the one and only God. Jesus is the connection; the link that reconnects humanity and God after man had been separated by sin. If we realize that we are truly connected, grafted in the Spirit of truth, reborn from above, then we must realize that God is listening to our prayers. The Apostle Paul prayed that we might know the hope of our calling. He was not saying that we should hope and then see what happens. He was saying, by the power of the Holy Spirit of God, that we *"know the hope."* It is a confident expectation in the results of prayer! If we pray, through the connecting line, Jesus Christ, know that the line is in service. There is no busy signal, God picks up, God cares! Do not let the devil convince us that God does not care. Satan's line is no longer is service because of his sin. However, Jesus dealt with our sin problem; He paid for our sins in full, with no balance remaining. If we ask God to forgive us, then we must change our thinking about the sin issue. All the prophets of old, all the apostles and Jesus Christ Himself, preached the power of repentance. God is faithful to forgive our sins because of the blood of Jesus that was sacrificed on the cross. If we repent, and begin to change our thinking, so as to resist the sins that prevent us from running by faith, than God is faithful and has given us the power by the Holy Spirit to be free from the sin that entangles us. This will happen through the power of prayer! Can we pray with a believing heart toward God? We can because God has given us His Spirit:

But when He, the Spirit of truth comes, He will guide you into all truth. John 16:13

What is Jesus saying? He is telling us that if the Spirit of God lives in us, He will teach us the truth through His word. If God is in the heart of a person, then he or she will begin to pray the prayers of faith. A prayer of faith can help so many people who otherwise would have no one praying for them at all.

I remember meeting a young boy at the playground while my son and I were playing ball. The young boy's name was Daniel and he would just sort of show up and ask to play. The Lord spoke to my heart one day when I was wondering why we kept meeting this kid at the playground. My heart told me that this little boy had no one praying for him. I have been praying for that boy ever since. God places these things in our hearts, and still gives us the choice whether to listen to our hearts or listen to our heads. So often, we choose to listen to our heads. Our so-called logical reasoning steps in the way of our faith. Now someone might say, what is wrong with logical thinking? Nothing, but God goes beyond our logic. Can we place God in our logical thinking? We seem to be convinced that God owes us all the explanations of why, who, when and how from the beginning of creation. God owes no one anything. The very life that is within us is a gift from God. It is not something that He owes us!

God tells us that faith is required, and it is not an option, but a requirement to enter the Kingdom of God.

Vessels of Mercy

And that He might make known the riches of His glory on the vessels of mercy, which he had prepared before hand for glory, even us whom He called, not of the Jews only, but also of the Gentiles? Romans 9:23 & 24

If we really want to run with God, if we really have a desire to know Him and if we want to understand His heart, then the above Scripture needs to take root into our hearts. If God has chosen to reveal His Son Jesus Christ to you and me, then it is important to know and fully understand the reason why we were called to live for the King of all kings. If we have truly found the risen Christ, and have given Him complete control, and all authority, then how can we walk in the darkness of sin? Instead, we should now please the one and only eternal God through His Son, Jesus Christ. If you have not found Jesus Christ as you Savior, then the next minute could be too late! The next breath or the next heartbeat could be your last here. If you are someone who does not have his or her eternal destiny reserved in Heaven by the power of the risen Christ, you are in danger. For there is no returning here once we leave these earthly bodies behind, until the day of the resurrection. No place in the Holy Scriptures does God say that we will return as other people or animals. God explains this that we pass through here once and once only! God does not promise reincarnation. He does promise us resurrection; some to be resurrected for judgment and some that are to be resurrected for eternal life in paradise. Jesus made this very clear when He said, *"I am the way" (John 14:6).* He did not say 'I know the way', or 'I have found the way.' If we want to capture the very meaning of this life and inherit the gift of eternal life, then know in your heart and mind that Jesus is the only way. Many religions have boasted to know the way to God, yet God Himself tells us clearly that Jesus Christ is the only way with no return visits until His return. If this issue cannot be settled in the heart and mind, the result is spiritual separation from God. This command does not come from religious leaders following a program of synthetic rituals. This command comes right from the mouth of God, written as a binding contract with the blood of Jesus Christ. Do not be fooled by empty promises of man. Read the word of God! *Jesus said to him, "I am the way, the truth and the life: no one comes to the Father but by me."* John 14:6 If someone has truly given God the Lordship of their life by surrendering all to Christ Jesus, then understand the position in which we were called. God calls us *vessels of mercy* and not vessels of wrath or accountants of God to keep track of everyone else's sin. We were not called to judge. I know it is not easy with the whispers of backbiters, proud boasters of self and deceitful people full of envy and strife. We know our first reaction in our flesh is we want God to destroy such people, but we remember *that while we were yet sinners, Christ died for us.* His mercy on us had nothing to do with our good behavior. It is pure grace! God can change us and is in the process of changing us in so many ways, but this is all done through His mercy. God wants us to be vessels of His love, to express His love in acts of mercy. If we think that because God has shown us the truth, we now have the right to judge the ungodly and even the godly, then we have no understanding in the love of God. God did not call us to be vessels of judgment.

It is so easy to criticize other people and point out their failures. It is so easy for us to turn our nose up and say that some are doomed. Let us make one fact completely clear in our minds, God in His never-ending love, loves the sinner. If He did not love the sinner, He would have never sent His Son to pay such an awesome price for the sins of the sinner. God has a problem with sin, because He is holy. But He has provided a solution for it. God has a cure for the infection called sin, and His name is Jesus. Do not bother looking for some other cure, some other way to touch God; your arm will be too short. Do not try to think that because there are so many other religions, that there are many ways to reach God, God says 'No!' He has provided a way of mercy, paved with grace that requires only faith to receive His promise. Out of faith, obedience will become a way to live in the presence of God. Do not fool yourself in thinking that one-day you or I will be good enough for the Kingdom of God. Our salvation is based upon the mercy of God, it is a gift. Our fallen nature stinks with the smell of sin. It is beyond us to remove the stain of sin, but God through His loving mercy, found a way.

There is no condemnation of those who are in Christ Jesus... Romans 8:1

God, who has shown us such an act of mercy, says to do the same and be vessels of His mercy to others.

Be merciful to those who doubt; snatch others from the fire and save them; to others show mercy, mixed with fear, hating even the clothing stained flesh. Jude 1:22, 23

God says to be merciful to an unbelieving world because there is no other hope for them to be saved without Christ. We might dislike some of the things that people do and say, but we were no different, and God's mercy is stronger than any sin. God calls every believer to be extensions of Him, and we know that the love He has for us was clearly displayed on the cross. God is willing to be merciful, and we ought to do the same.

It is very easy for the fan to sit on his couch, thinking that he or she could do a better job directing the team instead of the coach or the manager. However, when you are on the field things look a lot different than through a screen in slippers. It is the same in people's lives. It is easy to point a finger and suggest what they should have done, but when we could be in the same position, we might react the same way.

For by grace you have been saved through faith, and not of yourselves; it is a gift of God, not of works, lest anyone should boast. Ephesians 2:8

Throughout the Bible, we see repeatedly how God was merciful, even to His chosen people who would turn against Him, but even now, there is still a way back to Him with a more powerful promise than what the prophets of old had.

Now in Christ Jesus the blood of Christ has brought you who once were far off, near. Ephesians 2:13

The Knowledge of Him

We demolish arguments and every pretension that sets itself up against the knowledge of God and we take captive every thought to make it obedient to Christ.
2ⁿᵈ Corinthians 10:5

Paul, under the Spirit of God reveals several facts in this Scripture. The key words that stand out are, *arguments, thoughts,* and *obedient.* All have to do with the thinking element of man, his soul. The first fact that God brings to light is that there are no *arguments* against God. For with all the science and theories that man has tried to disprove the very existence of God, has failed. They can say that this explosion or that collision formed the universe. However, the question will always be where did the matters that exploded or collided come from? There will be no answer except that God created it. The second key word is *thought.* It is clearly in a person's thinking that decides whether to do good or evil. Now with this logical thought, we try to dismiss or disprove God according to what has been programmed in our minds. We will always try to relate present findings with past experiences. This is reasonable with other things, but not with the knowledge of God. The third key word is *obedient.* A word most people do not like because most of us are rebels by nature. *Obedient* is just another word for submission. Therefore, our *arguments* come from *thoughts* and our obedience comes from *thoughts.* The choices are clearly given by God. The first choice is that we can rebel, raise arguments against the knowledge of God. We have the ability to walk our thoughts away from knowing God, since no one is twisting any arms. If we have not received His salvation, then we need to consider all the facts, all the proof that God is very real and invites us to know Him. This invitation is not just for these few years here that seem to race by day after day, year after year. This invitation is for an eternal existence in the presence of the one and only Creator, and this is in the *knowledge of God.*

But God demonstrates His own love for us in this: while we were still sinners, Christ died for us.
Romans 5:8

We can argue, or we can believe. All is in the choice of our thoughts. The question is this: Who is influencing our thoughts? Some people might say that they are not influenced by anything or anybody, that they have a mind of their own. Well that is true; God did give us a mind and a free will to choose right from wrong. However, something or somebody has influenced every one of us in the past, and those experiences begin to develop a thought pattern. This thought pattern affects the decisions that we make now. The other factor that helps us make decisions and sets our thought patterns is knowledge. Now if you are a professional, then you have gained knowledge, with experience and by formal training, you know how to do your job. That is called knowledge and that will affect your pattern of thinking. Another good example of this is the person who is interested in a certain occupation. Let us say the occupation chosen is a computer programmer. Now if this person has no, or very limited knowledge and experience on a computer, they will certainly not know how to program the system. This will also affect their decisions, their judgment in even attempting to program a computer; they are lost until they gain some knowledge on how to program. However, the knowledge of God is more than just knowledge; it is an understanding of who He is in a relationship with Him. Unlike the knowledge of programming a computer, this takes more than just the natural mind; understanding God takes a union in spirit, it takes our hearts. It is a fusion of the creation being crafted together with the Creator. It requires the use of our hearts along with our minds. We cannot know God from a distant knowledge, but by a personal relationship with Him.

In Him we have redemption through His blood, the forgiveness of sins, in accordance with the riches of God's grace that He lavished on us with all wisdom and understanding.
Ephesians 1:7

A Touch of Faith

At once Jesus realized that the power had gone out from Him. He turned around in the crowd and asked, "Who is touching Me?" Mark 5:30

We learn about a woman who the Bible tells us was subject to bleeding for twelve years. That is a lot of bleeding. For twelve years this women suffered from a flow of blood that not only drained her physically, but also brought her mental suffering as well. God tells us that she was under the care of many doctors and had to spend all she had to find a cure. However, no doctors that treated her could stop the bleeding; all the money she spent on trying to find a doctor to cure her did not help. Moreover, after twelve years of bleeding, going to doctor after doctor, spending all she had, the condition was even getting worse. She had faith in her money, thinking she could afford the best doctors. She had placed her faith in the doctors thinking that one of them will find a cure, only to come up empty and getting worse.

She had exhausted all the other hopes and then someone told her about Jesus. The word about Jesus was spreading fast. Could He be the Savior who Israel had been waiting for? She heard about a Man that heals blind eyes, deaf ears, crippled bodies, and raises the dead. Now when she heard these things she could have said, 'I'll ask my doctor to see what he thinks about this Jesus.' On the other hand, she could have said, 'I'll go ask my priest about the man Jesus and see what he has to say.' Alternatively, she could have decided to turn on the news to see what the experts said about this Man Jesus. This woman knew that the doctors had no answers, and the priest gave her no hope, in fact, the priest would have condemned her, saying that it was because God was angry with her. As far as the experts go, they talk in circles because they do not know the answers. Instead, this woman went right to Jesus. She had nothing else to lose. She tried everything else and all failed. Therefore, she made a plunge for Jesus. Do we need to try all the other options before we come to God? This woman had tried everything else; she had nothing else to lose, so she took a leap of faith.

When she heard about Jesus, she came up behind Him in the crowd and touched His cloak, because she thought, "If I just touch His clothes, I will be healed."
Mark 5:27

The women never heard Jesus speak as far as we know; she never saw His face. The text does not say that she saw any other miracles that Jesus performed. God tells us that she only *heard about Jesus*. Then when she touched His garment, the blood stopped immediately and she was healed.

Have you heard about Jesus? Are you looking for an opinion from your doctor? Do you believe what they are telling you on news? I can tell you that before your situation becomes hopeless, before you have tried all the other opinions of doctors, religious leaders, or the experts on the news, try Jesus. Take a step of faith toward God who cannot resist a prayer in faith. God, the Creator, who created the universe, the planets, the sun and His finest creation, namely us, can also heal a body, a mind, or a broken spirit. He is, after all, the One who made us. One touch of faith, one trust in the Son of God will mend the broken, heal the hurt, and save the lost. Jesus is waiting; you do not need anyone else to go to Him. He is waiting with open arms, and hands with holes that say, "I love you." God truly loves us not because we are perfect, not because we never do anything wrong, and not because we never sin. It was out of His love that God created us and out of His mercy that He saves us. He loves us because we are His creation, as any good parent loves their child. Touch Jesus with a prayer of faith and you will hear Him speak to your heart and say:

"...Don't be afraid; just believe."
Mark 5:36

An Offering

And then Moses spoke to all the congregation of the children of Israel saying, "This is the thing which the Lord commanded saying: Take from among you an offering to the Lord. Whoever is of a willing heart, let him bring it as an offering to the Lord. Then everyone whose heart was stirred, and everyone whose spirit was willing, brought the Lord's offering for the work of the Tabernacle of Meeting, for the Holy Garment.
Exodus 35:4 & 5, 35:21

God commands Moses to assemble His people in one place, let us call it the church; Moses calls it the Tabernacle of Meeting. In this Tabernacle, His people could worship, sing, and pray with one heart and one mind to the one and only God. It was a place where God could manifest His presence. God now asked for an offering for the service of the Tabernacle. Moses, whose ministry was not only to lead God's chosen people out of Egypt, but also to bring this chosen race into a relationship with God begins to ask the people for an offering. Already God begins the teaching of His principles concerning the blessings in giving. Here God also gives us a view of that first congregation and the mission of Moses. I believe that when God saw Moses willing to risk all the wealth and position he had in Egypt, God saw a man who was willing to place other people in front of himself. Moses, who had all that the world had to offer, was willing to throw it all away because of his compassion. He could not stand by while someone was being abused. Moses was willing! In the verse above, Moses explains the condition needed for the giving of an offering...*a willing heart* for the Lord. Not perfection, not man's knowledge, and not some kind of self-strength, God says you need a *willing heart,* a merciful heart. If your heart is willing, God will do the rest. Moses begins to minister to this chosen race the things that God was revealing to him.

The children of Israel brought a freewill offering to the Lord, all the men and women whose hearts were willing to bring material for all kinds of work which the Lord, by the hand of Moses, had commanded to be done.
Exodus 35:29
God is looking for the willingness in our hearts to use us as vessels of mercy. The free will offering, given not out of a requirement or obligation, but out of a desire to please God, is a wonderful gift within itself. God gives us an opportunity to offer something back to Him. After all, God is the one who gives all things to us. Imagine being able to give something to God.

God shows His mercy even to the ungrateful. Just think how kind He is to the ones who are grateful and willing to give. He is looking for a *willing heart* to give the same way Jesus gave all He had to us. God, who loved us before the foundation of the world, who even shares His very being with us, will bless the *willing heart*. God, who gives us the gift of eternal life and who allows the sun to rise on the grateful and the ungrateful, teaches us to give. Moreover, God who is rich in mercy and kindness continues to shower us with the gifts of His love.

Every good gift and every perfect gift is from above, and comes down from the Father of lights, with whom is no variables, neither shadow of turning.
James 1:17
Now Moses writes that all who were willing brought a freewill offering unto the Lord. Moses does not write all were willing. That leads me to believe that some did not have a willing heart to give. We need to understand that when God is going to do something, He is going to do it whether we participate or not. If God only found one willing heart, He would still succeed in what He wants to do.

Then something very interesting happens with the building of the sanctuary.

...And the people continued to bring free will offerings morning after morning. Then Moses gave an order and they sent this word through out the camp: "no man or woman is to make anything else as an offering or the sanctuary." Therefore, the

people were restrained from bringing more, because what they already had was more than enough to do all the work.
Exodus 36: 2, 6&7

Can you imagine an assembly of people who had such willing hearts to give, that the leader finally had to restrain them and say, no more, we have more than enough?

A generous man will prosper; he who refreshes others will himself be refreshed
Proverbs11: 25

"And if anyone gives even a cup of cold water to one of these little ones because he is My disciple, I tell you the truth, he will certainly not lose his reward."
Matthew 10 42

Honor the Lord with your wealth, with the first fruits of all your crops, then your barns will be filled to overflowing, and your vats will brim over with new wine.
Proverbs 3: 9,10

"Give, and it shall be given to you: good measure, pressed down, and shaken together, and running over, shall men give to you. For with the same measure that you give it shall be measured to you again."
Luke 6:38

It is in the willing heart where God can do His greatest work. And in that willingness, there is a peace that surpasses the fears of lack that overrides the doubts of His provision, and gives us a clearer understanding of His eternal mercy toward us.

For the Lord is good; His mercy is everlasting, and His truth endures to all generations.
Psalm 100: 5

Return to Me

Therefore tell the people this is what the Lord Almighty said, "Return to Me," declares the Lord Almighty. "And I will return to you," said the Lord Almighty.
Zechariah 1:3

If there was ever a message given by God as to call a nation of people out of their captivity of sin, Zechariah received one. Although this message was delivered to the people of Israel, it is also delivered to all nations today. God tells us to return to Him. The key word *return* is defined as come back, or give back and in the above message God is asking for both. Come back to Him as following His love, His word, His mercy, and give back to Him the honor and love from our hearts that He alone deserves as the Creator of all life. Return to the child-like faith that cannot be tossed by the waves of doubt that gives birth to confusion and uncertainty. Return to His word that covers us like a shield of power against the darkness of evil. We now have something far greater than the people did in Zechariah's day. They had the prophets in that God would speak through them, but we have the witness of God's Spirit, the Holy Spirit who speaks to each one of us, and lives in our beings.

He will give you another Helper, that He may abide with you forever, the Spirit of Truth, Whom the world cannot receive because it neither sees Him nor knows Him, but you know Him, for He dwells with you and will be in you.
John 14:16 - 17

The Holy Spirit is revealed as the *Spirit of truth* and *another Helper*. In the days of Zechariah, the people had forsaken the truth for the worship of dead objects. This is still true for the world today; some even call money the almighty dollar. God reveals His heart to the prophet as He extends His offer of love and said, *"Return to Me."* The offer still stands, but now with even a more powerful witness, the Holy Spirit, and with a stronger promise based on the mercy of His love and not on the letter of the law.

I will not leave you orphans. I will come to you.
John 14:18

143

*Father, the hour has come. Glorify your Son, that your Son
also may glorify you, as you have given Him authority over all
flesh, that He should give eternal life to as many as you have
given Him.*
John 17:1 and 2
We have powerful promises that many in past times did not
have, but with the same request from God, *"Return to Me."*
Return; come back to Him with our minds renewed by His love
for us. Return; give back to Him our love, our thankfulness to
the one and only Creator, and to His endless miracles. The
offer remains, extended to all, to be received in faith. There are
no other conditions, no small print, and no clauses in the
binding contract (The New Covenant) that was signed in blood.
We need to remember what happened to Israel repeatedly, as
they strayed from God to worship the works of their own hands.
God makes an awesome promise, a written guarantee that
says, *"Return to Me and I will return to you."* Every one of us is
only one prayer away to a closer relationship with God. It is the
key that unlocks the door; the prayer in faith according to the
promise and the submission to His will. Return to the Lord and
begin to live in His mercy.
Jesus gives us the greatest illustration of God's mercy when
someone returns to Him in the parable of the prodigal son. The
wayward son, who had wasted all the valuable riches given
from his father, finds himself alone with nothing. This story told
by the Master has the most powerful example of God's love
toward us. We all have heard this story repeatedly, but it could
never be told enough.
Then He said, "A certain man had two sons."
*The younger son gathered, journeyed to a far country, and
there wasted his possessions with prodigal living.*
Luke 15:11 and 13
This is a true illustration of our spiritual rebellion against God.
Just as this father had given a rebellious son an inheritance of
physical wealth, God has given us (every believer), all His
spiritual wealth in the powerful bank account of faith. Our
spiritual wealth is the same as the young son's physical wealth

that was given freely as a birth right inheritance that he did not earn, and neither did we.

Blessings follow obedience, and correction will follow rebellion, but all done in love, and then there is mercy.

The father in the story gave to his son out of love, although the son took his father's love for granted. Do we take God's love for granted? This story will certainly raise some questions in our hearts. Nevertheless, the father in the story gives, and the son wasted what was given. God has given us the gift of life, the gift to love and the powerful gift of faith. Like the young son, do we just waste it on our selfish ambitions? The wayward son could have used his given wealth to help others, to support his father in obedience, which in turn would have increased his inheritance, but had chosen to waste it on himself. This is a powerful message to every believer who no longer thinks they have anything to give to other people or to God. Then the son falls into the sea of sorrows with no food, no home, no love, and alone. He is hungry (as many of us were, or still are), and in spiritual darkness because we lost sight of His hope. Then this son remembers his father's house. He recalls his father's mercy whereas even the hired men were well fed and paid. At that moment, he realizes his sin and decides that he will humble himself before his father even to the point of being a hired servant.

When we realize our sin, when we see clearly that we were rebels against God and had taken the valuable gift of life for granted, wasting it on our own selfish ambitions and pleasures, then we will also humbly return to God.

When the son returned to his father something supernatural happened:

But when he was still a great way off, his father saw him and had compassion, and ran and fell on his neck and kissed him. Luke 15:20

What a powerful illustration of God's mercy and His love. While we also were far off in a dead, comatose spiritual condition, in a wasteland, God saw us while we were coming to Him, and He embraced us with His compassion.

...For your brother was dead and is alive again, and was lost and is found.
Luke 16:32
We all have strayed in the blindness of spiritual darkness, stumbling in the lukewarm state of faith. While we were in that state, God saw us far off and ran to us with open arms just as the father had welcomed back the son who wasted his life.
For this my son was dead and is alive again; he was lost and is found. And they began to be merry. Luke 15:24
As the son in the story started a journey home, to the place where he knew his father was in control, so we journey to eternal life with God. The journey begins when we realize, like this son in the story; we are stumbling in the darkness of defeat without the direction of the Father, just as the son had made poor decisions that left him in a sea of sorrows. I believe that this was no casual walk. It was a passionate run to his father because of his hunger, his loneliness, his emptiness, and his knowing that he would perish without the help of his dad. As the father in the story allowed his young son to make his own decisions and his own mistakes, but was waiting for the day that his son would return to him by his own free will, so God waits for anyone who has drifted away from His love.
Jesus gives us a great insight of the mercy of God as we see the joy of the father who has back the son whom he had lost and a son who found the true riches of life in the love of his father.
"I will heal their backsliding, I will love them freely..."
Hosea 14: 4

The Fuel of Faith

The Lord had said to Abram, "Leave your country, your people and your father's household and go to the land I will show you." *Genesis 12:1*

Abraham, (Abram) was told by God to leave the security of his father's house, leave all the friends that welcomed him, and leave the familiar countryside. Isaac wondered from place to place, digging wells until he settled in the place called Rehoboth. Jacob was forced to flee from his brother. Joseph was kidnapped and sold in a strange land called Egypt. There for many years he found no home, but a jail cell was his residence. Then we find Moses, the baby given up for survival and ends up in a king's palace. Moses grows up, kills a man and then we see him on the run, a run of faith.

There is a common thread with all of these men. God led them all into unknown lands and removed the security blanket of home ground. Moreover, all of them had no idea what was going to happen next. When stripped of their security, their safe zone of home surroundings, loving friends, family, and a daily routine, they started to run a journey of faith. The word of God tells us that faith is the driving force behind the move of God. Like the electricity for a machine or gasoline for a motor, faith is the fuel. There is victory and power in trusting God

Now since God is the source of faith, the Author of our faith, then He alone can inject us with it. However, just like any motor or any machine, the parts must be first properly assembled in working order to be able to use the source of power. I believe that in all of the prophet's lives, God was busy assembling the parts in these men to use the fuel of faith in them and through them, and God will do the same for us. This is not to say that God will take all of us from our familiar surroundings. However, when we read about the lives of these men, we can see that most of the time they had been placed in some very uncomfortable positions. Sometimes in our comfort zone, we are unable to use the very thing that moves God called faith. In this comfort zone, we can find contentment, but lose the hunger for God. We can become so content with an easy life, and forget the very purpose of our existence.

God does not tell everyone to go to an unknown country and leave everything else behind. Nevertheless, He does command us to crown Him the absolute King and Lord of our lives, (submission) and sometimes that is even more than uncomfortable. Moses had all the comforts in Egypt. After all, he was raised in a palace. I think most of us could become very content with that, especially if we had been raised in that surrounding. Therefore, if we become comfortable, so content with our day-to-day existence, then a good meal and an easy chair replace the hunger for God. God took these men of old off their couch, took the remote control out of their hands and began to work the parts in their lives. Only then, could the fuel of faith be injected and ignited into a fire for God in their hearts. The real objective was to use these men for the divine purpose of leading others to God.

When do our prayers become the most sincere? When are our cries to God the loudest? When our bellies are full with our feet up watching the tube? I do not think so. However, talk to someone whose life is up side down and has no idea what will become of their situation tomorrow. If that person is a true believer in God, they will confess, 'I have no choice, but to trust God.' God will put us in uncomfortable situations to bring us closer to Him and to fulfill His eternal purpose for our lives. The closer we get to Him, the less our present situation seems to matter. Moses, Abraham, Jacob, and Joseph were all positioned in very uncomfortable places, every one of them had to come to a dead end, and say; 'I'm going to trust God.'

I believe that in that state of submission is where God can do the greatest work in us. The parts are then assembled, the fuel of faith is injected, and the mighty hand of God is moved by faith. God cannot resist faith. God is drawn to faith like a magnet to steel. Trusting Him brings us closer and closer to Him. Once the fire of faith is burning, God cannot help but see the flame. However, if we are trying to fill our bellies and our wants with materialism instead of feeding our spirits with the truth, the fire of faith will only spark occasionally. So how do we begin a journey of faith? How do we turn a spark in to a fire? God tells us how!

So then faith comes by hearing, and hearing by the word of God. Roman 10:17

Therefore, faith is the fuel that sets us on fire for God, and the word of God is the fuel source for faith. Faith increases by digesting the word of God; a steady diet of Gods word will build faith. When we can begin to know God's word and trust it, then we know God. Now God is not talking about just reading, memorizing and quoting His word, God wants us to apply it to our every day lives. You know the old phrase, 'if God said it; I believe it and that settles it!' While we believe, and trust in God's word, our faith will grow as a deep routed tree, unable to be moved by the many storms in this life. As we apply the word of God to our everyday lives, all the parts of a faith machine are in the process of assembly. It is not going to matter what the world is doing or what the world is selling. If it does not line up with Gods word, then forget it. Abraham believed God when he was too old to have a son. Joseph, buried in a prison cell knew that God was his only hope. Moses met God on a mountaintop, and believed when God told him to go set His people free. On and on we could go, from King David to the Apostles, men and women of faith that moved the hand of God, because they trusted His word and surrendered their lives to it. By this act of submission to God in faith, the mercy of God was always with them.

Then He (Jesus), *touched their eyes and said, "According to your faith will it be done to you," and their sight was restored. Matthew 9:29*

Jesus told the two blind men, *"According to your faith."* Little faith, then there is little movement from God. Big faith, and look out.

Strong faith will bring God's power into the picture every time.

Justified by Mercy

Two men went up to the temple to pray, one a Pharisee and the other a tax collector. The Pharisee stood up and prayed about himself: "God, I thank you that I am not like other men, robbers, evildoers, adulterers, or even like this tax collector. I fast twice a week and give a tenth of all I get! The tax collector stood at a distance. He would not even look up to Heaven, but beat his breast and said, 'God have mercy on me, a sinner!'
Luke 18:10 -- 13

What a great illustration Jesus gives on how powerful the mercy of God prevails. Here we see a Pharisee; he was a teacher of the law and a well-respected man. He was not only a teacher of the law, but he was supposed to be a spiritual leader. This man was very well educated and very sure his so-called sacrifices would impress God. However, he seemed to forget that he had sinned somewhere in his life. He starts to boast of how he never stole or how he never committed adultery. Did that impress God? Maybe he never had a temptation to steal, maybe he never was with another woman except for his wife, but God says, "*All have sinned and fall short of the Glory of God.*" That means that this Pharisee had sinned and that would mean he owed a payment for sin. He stands before God in prayer saying, 'I am better than this tax collector.' Did not that Pharisee know that all sin stinks with the same foul odor to God? Whether it is the murder of an unborn child or a little white lie, it is all sin to God.

God does not have levels of sin; it is all the same. The real definition of sin is simply disobedience to God; there is no other definition of sin. God says, 'do not do that' and we do it anyway, it is sin. Therefore, the Pharisee stands before God in prayer with his nose up in the air, telling God how great he is. By what the Lord tells us in the next verse, God was not very happy with his self-righteousness. It sounds as if the Pharisee was going to be judged very strongly before God. On the other hand, here comes the tax collector. They were considered sinners because most of them stole, cheated, and lied when collecting money. This tax collector comes in the presence of God with his head bowed low and with a humble heart. The tax collector, who was no expert of the law, knew and understood the mercy of God. He knew enough about sin to know that it is all the same and if we break one commandment, we have broken them all. Therefore, this tax collector found the secret that the Pharisee in all his so-called knowledge had overlooked. God forgives, God redeems, God renews and God justifies by the acts of His mercy.

We cannot be justified by how many good things we do. However, God is a merciful Creator. We are redeemed, forgiven, and accepted by the One who commanded us life from our mother's womb. That is not to say that we will not have to live out the consequences in our daily decisions. It does mean that God is merciful to those who are willing to humble themselves before God and ask for mercy, through forgiveness, and are willing to change. It is not based on how good we behave, or based on who we are, but based on who God is, because He is love.

For who can undo a wrong from yesterday? If someone spills their drink on the ground, it is gone, no recovery. When a mother decides to give up her unborn child to the hand of the abortionist, who can bring that child back once their gone? We cannot undo our sins from the past. We can only live that day once, although in our memories, some days seem to replay repeatedly. The tax collector knew he could not change yesterday, yesterday was gone, and the future holds many questions, although we can only capture the present by learning from the past. We cannot live anywhere else except in the present, but we have an eternal hope in the future. The self-righteous, highly educated, well-respected teacher of law knew nothing about the mercy of God. Therefore, he missed the most important part. He missed the most revealing part of God's very nature, because he was too busy judging other people and praising himself.

For everyone who exalts himself will be humbled, and he who humbles himself will be exalted. Luke 18:14

God is the one who exalts; God is the one who gives honor. The world can give a person position, respected titles, and new suits to accompany it, but the inward man is still decayed with self-interest, resulting in self-righteousness, blinded by the sight of ourselves, and the mercy of God is missed without Christ. *The greatest among you will be your servant. Matthew 23:12* God is looking for the humble heart because in that heart He can do His greatest work. After all, are we able to pay for our own sins? What can we do to wash away the stain of sin like a grease mark on a white sheet? What bleach do we have that is strong enough to wash ourselves clean? None! If that was the case, if somehow we could redeem ourselves by good works, then Jesus went to the cross in vain. The heart of Christianity is the cross. Without it, there is no redemption. Can we make up for past mistakes? Can we justify a wrong by saying, 'I did something wrong, but now I am going to make it right?' With some situations in life, it may appear that we resolve some of our errors, but when it comes to sin, once it is done, it stains. I wonder how my spirit must have looked, full of the dark stains of sin? Now I can say, I have been washed clean, not by so-called acts of self-righteousness, but by the blood of my Savior, Jesus Christ. He had no stains on His garment, no sin, yet was willing to put on my garment, full of stains, and wore it on the cross to wash me clean. I am cleansed, not by my self-righteousness, not by my will power to resist evil, not by justifying my sin, but by the grace and mercy of God in Jesus Christ.

"Salvation is found in no one else, for there is no other name under Heaven given to men by which we are to by saved."
Acts 4:26

You can look high and low, east to west, north to south, you can look to men with promises, men with theories and philosophies, but without the stain removing, sin forgiving, power of God by the blood of Jesus Christ, we are lost in a sea of sin and judgment.

Activate Your Faith

Nevertheless, the righteous will live by his faith.
"If you have faith as small as a mustard seed, nothing will be
impossible for you." Habakkuk 2: 4, Matthew 17:20
Faith, what is it? Faith is the hope of things unseen. Can you
see your salvation? Nevertheless, by believing the promise of
God we are saved from eternal separation from God.
In the letter from Paul to the Romans, God's Spirit explains how
Abraham trusted the word of God in the promise to be a father
of many nations. How could Abraham be a father at all? He had
no children with his wife Sarah. Abraham was advanced in
years; he was ninety-nine years old!
Without weakening in his faith, he faced the fact that his body
was as good as dead. Since he was about one hundred years
old, and Sarah's womb was also dead. Yet, he did not waiver
through unbelief regarding the promise of God.
Romans 4:19, 20
Abraham believed and trusted God, he cast out any doubts he
had within himself and stayed focused on the promise.
Abraham lived by faith. Moses and all the prophets also
believed and trusted God at His word. Since God is truth, there
should be no question that what he says will come true. Our
Lord Jesus rebuked some for their lack of faith and praised
others for their abundance of faith, but as we can see through
out the Scriptures, faith moves the hand of God. In the gospels,
we see how Jesus showed us what the power of faith in God
could do.

Jesus turned and saw her "Take heart daughter," He said,
"Your faith has healed you." Then He touched their eyes and
said, "According to your faith will it be done to you," and their
sight was restored. Jesus said to the woman, "Your faith has
saved you, go in peace." Then He said to him, "Rise and go;
your faith has made you well." Matthew 9:22, Matthew 9:29, 30
Luke 7:50, Luke 17:19

Why are we in such a hurry to trust the accountants, financial
advisors, doctors and even people in our day to day lives and
are so slow to trust in the one and only living God, who without

Him there would be nothing? How can we put our trust in the things of this world instead of the living God who created it? *Show me your faith without deeds and I will show you my faith by what I do. James 2:18*
Activating faith is an action, a decision in standing on the word of truth, believing God in what He promises. Now you can own many things in this world like a car, but if you never drive it, what good will it do? It is the same with faith, if God has given you faith He expects you to use it in every situation of our lives. And when we do use it, God's promises will happen and in the process, we will also become closer to God.
And the Scripture was fulfilled that says, "Abraham believed God, and it was credited to Him as righteousness," and He was called God's friend. James 2:23
You can take all this world has to offer and multiply it repeatedly and it would never compare to being a friend of God. It begins and ends in faith.
Everything that does not come from faith is sin. Romans 14:23
When the unbeliever stands up to say, "I have lived a good life, I have never murdered or stole, I have been faithful to my wife, I do not lie or curse, smoke or drink." If he has done all these things without faith in God, he has missed the mercy of God through faith and is still with sin.
For in the gospel a righteousness from God is revealed, a righteousness that by faith from first to last, just as it is written: the righteous will live by faith. Romans 1:17
By faith Noah, when warned about things not yet seen, in holy fear built and ark to save his family. Hebrews 11:7
Faith in the Son of God can bring healing, deliverance, spiritual understanding and vision. Faith can tear down the walls of division and build foundations of unity.

The Profit

"For what will it profit a man if he gains the whole world, and loses his own soul?" Mark 8:3
In the above Scripture, we are asked an important question: What will it profit a man if he loses his own soul? Not lose financial security, not lose a job, not lose the ball game, God is saying that it is very possible to lose our souls. Therefore, we can fulfill every desire we might have on this earth, and live a life full of pleasure; with all the things the world can offer, and then find out, we have missed the mercy of God. If we lose our soul, there is no profit. If we miss God's mercy, there is only a very big loss!
King Solomon had all his eyes desired. He writes that he withheld nothing that he wanted, but at the end of his journey, he confesses, *"It is all vanity."* All the earthy wealth, all the pleasures, all the lust and all the power that he had was all in vain, without God. Moreover, at the end of a lavish lifestyle, Solomon tells us to *"Seek God."* For all that he had, he had nothing without the Lord God.
And then we come to eternity. Once we leave here, there is no turning back! Is anyone willing to take that chance? Are we willing to trade the few sinful things this world can offer for eternity? What are we going to say when we stand before the Almighty, the Creator of heaven and earth, God Himself?
I know what some people are going to tell God on that day. They will justify themselves and say how good they were. However, God will reply:
For all have sinned, and come short of the glory of God. Romans 3:23
All have sinned; I think that includes you and I. No one who has sinned will be glorified in the presence of God unless their sins have been forgiven, washed clean. Can we be forgiven by weighing the scale of justice and comparing our so-called good deeds, to how many sins we have committed against God, and somehow think that we can be justified on our own merit? The answer is no, because just one sin is enough to fall from the glory of God.
For the wages of sin is death. Romans 6:23

So what can we do? We know that there is a God who created the heavens and the earth. We know that this life is temporary and that we are all leaving, we just do not know when. We also know that we have all sinned; therefore, we have all earned the wages of death! What are we to do?

For the wages of sin is death; but the gift of God is eternal life through Jesus Christ our Lord. Romans 6:23

The wages, judgment *of sin is death*, which means that although some of us are still breathing through these bodies, and are above the ground, if our sins are not paid for, then we are dead. Maybe not physically yet, but spiritually dead, separated from God.

Now the blood of God's Son was sinless; therefore, He was the only person that could ever pay such a price. No other human, whether a so-called prophet, or any religious leader could ever make this claim except for Jesus Christ. This cannot be repeated enough.

Notice how God calls eternal life with Him, *a gift*. You cannot work for a gift, for then it would be a wage, as we worked for sin, and the wage for that is death. A gift is given free, no charge, not earned, but given. However, even a gift has to be received. God put out His hands and had them nailed to a cross to prevent us from losing our souls for eternity.

Now many people are under the impression that if they ever truly gave everything to God, that they would lose all the things they love. They think that somehow they will become some kind of robotic believer that is programmed to say and do only what the leaders of the church command. It is not about the church leaders, they are only men and women that have the same faults that are in all of us. It is not what man says or demands, but it is about a relationship with God, through Jesus Christ. Of course, a good church leader is more like a shepherd who is a caretaker for God's flock. God is not looking for robots, because if He was, He could have easily made us that way. Robots can perform a function, but they cannot love, and since God is love, love is what He wants from us, because love is a choice. Can all the riches in the earth buy love? How many times have we seen wealthy and famous people drown themselves in abuse because they are lacking love? What profit did they gain even in this short life? Without the love of God, which can only come from a relationship through Jesus Christ, *all is vanity*. Therefore, there is no greater *profit* for any living soul than to have a relationship with Jesus Christ. That relationship will bring us to abide in the love of God, which will also take us through this life into the presence of God, and that is by far the best place we could ever be! God is not looking to take away the good things in life, but wants us to have the very best thing, and that is the knowledge of His love in the person of Jesus Christ. Once anyone has experienced God's love through Christ, all the other stuff that seemed so important to us now is small change, pennies, because the love of God is by far the true wealth of this life, and moreover, the life to come. What could be better than that?

Jesus said:

Behold, I stand at the door and knock; if any man hears my voice, and open the door, I will come in to Him... Revelations 3:20

This is between you and God.

In your own words, from your heart, ask God by the power of the sacrifice of Jesus Christ to forgive your past sins. Explain to God that you are deeply sorry for every sin that you ever committed, and ask Him to renew your heart with His love. And by faith, accept the free gift of the sacrifice of Jesus Christ on the cross for your sin. For if anyone truly believes that Jesus Christ died on the cross for every sin they committed, and was raised on the third day, and openly confesses this truth, they have eternal life. Then ask Jesus to come into your heart, and make Him Lord over your life, because Jesus promised that if anyone opens the door of their hearts to Him, He will come into those hearts.

It is only after accepting God's gift that we can walk with Him through this life and know that we will be with Him for eternity. Read God's word, find a church that is Scripture based, and most of all, pray! Pray to the only Creator of heaven and earth to reveal His will for your life and thank Him everyday for His gift to us, Jesus Christ.

"For God so loved the world that He gave (a gift), *His only begotten Son, that whoever* (regardless of color, race, age or past sins), *believes in Him* (Jesus Christ) *should not perish but have everlasting life* (an endless eternity in the loving presence of God)."*
John 3:16

Scripture references taken from the following:

King James Version Bible
New King James Version Bible
New American Standard Bible
Williams Version Bible – In the language of the people
Beck Version Bible – In the language of today
New living Translation Version Bible
New International Version Bible
Revised Standard Version Bible

This book is dedicated to Jesus Christ, our Lord and Savior by the power of the Holy Spirit, to the glory of God the Father, and to all the saints who have been washed in the Lamb's blood. May His mercy reign in our hearts, refresh our minds and cause our spirits to grow in the knowledge of His love.

Special thanks to Joyce Flynn for all her help.